From the Killing Fields of Cambodia…

Through Fields of Grace

Lakhina L. Brown

"…*If only I may finish the race and complete the task
the Lord Jesus has given me—*
the task of testifying to the gospel of God's grace…"
(Acts 20:24).

Copyright © 2007 by Lakhina L. Brown

Through Fields of Grace
by Lakhina L. Brown
A Legacy of Hope International Publication

Printed in the United States of America

ISBN 978-1-60266-033-5

All rights reserved solely by the author. The author guarantees all contents are original and do not infringe upon the legal rights of any other person or work. This book or parts thereof may not be reproduced in any form, stored in a retrieval system, or transmitted in any form by any means— electronic, mechanical, photocopy, recording, or otherwise— without prior written permission of the author, except as provided by United States of America copyright law. The views expressed in this book are not necessarily those of the publisher.

Scriptures quotations are taken from the NIV Study Bible. Copyright © 1985 by The Zondervan Corporation. The Holy Bible, New International Version® Copyright © 1973, 1978, 1984 by International Bible Society. Used by permission of Zondervan Publishing House. All rights reserved.

For booking information or
to schedule a speaking engagement please contact:

Legacy of Hope International
P.O. Box 490147
Leesburg, FL 34749
Web Site: www.LOHIntl.org
E-Mail: info@lohintl.org

Cover photo by Steven T. Brown, and Allen Tedder with Design Prophets
Photo of girls face was taken by Photographer - Maciej Dakowicz

www.xulonpress.com

CONTENTS

Dedication ix
Foreword xi
Acknowledgments xiii
Introduction xv

Chapter 1:   The Great Fall 17
Chapter 2:   Through the Killing Fields 27
Chapter 3:   Through Valleys of Death 37
Chapter 4:   Launching for Liberty 47
Chapter 5:   Jesus in the Refugee Camp 55
Chapter 6:   Farewell My Hero and Homeland! 65
Chapter 7:   The Land of the Living 75
Chapter 8:   The Ultimate Betrayal 89
Chapter 9:   Where Do I Belong? 97
Chapter 10: Angels Unaware 105
Chapter 11: A Deal with the Devil 115
Chapter 12: Set Apart 125
Chapter 13: Instrument of Wickedness 131
Chapter 14: Death into Dancing 143
Chapter 15: Choose Life 155

A Tribute to My King:

I was shattered, submerged in sorrows,
My Lord! You surged my heart with joy.

Covered in shame, clothed with disgrace,
My God! You cleansed me from filthy stains.

Hopelessly wretched and hunted by death,
My Savior! You snatched me from the grave.

Dead in my transgressions, a lifeless corpse,
My Redeemer! You gave me breath of life.

Because of Your intoxicating love for me,
My Father! I now love.

Who else do I have in heaven or on earth?
Oh, Magnificent Master, But You,
The Author of my every breath!

Lakhina Brown

DEDICATION

I dedicate this book to the three people most responsible for my being alive: God, my father and my mother. God, if it was not for you, I would not exist, let alone this book. How can I ever begin to express my gratitude to you for all the wonders and miracles that you have performed in my life? You are the author of my life, and the breath of my being.

Father, how proud I am to have your valiant blood coursing through my veins. Although our lives together have been tragically interrupted, your faithfulness and bravery as a courageous military commander gave me strength despite costing you your life. I am honored to have your fierce tiger-spirit as my inheritance.

Mother, I know no woman on earth who is stronger and braver than you. Thank you for carrying me through. When life was at its darkest hour your strength and courage shone like the noonday sun. Although we missed twenty-five years of life together, the God who preserved our lives from death has already begun to restore all that was lost. May our Redeemer be glorified with the remaining years of our lives. Thank you for helping me to preserve our family's heritage within the pages of *Through Fields of Grace*.

FOREWORD

Few father-in-laws have the privilege of getting to know their daughter in-law like I know Lakhina. Despite living in different states along the eastern coast of the United States, we have spent what I would consider a typical amount of time together. However, for the past several months I have been helping her to refine her life's story in this, her first book. It describes the incredible journey of one of millions of children caught up in the madness of the Cambodian Killing Fields.

As my work on this book progressed, I teased Lakhina that I had been able to climb into both her head and her heart. I said this because, as she told her story, it wasn't long before I actually began to sense what she was feeling and experience what she was experiencing. It was as though I was actually there.

Fear is one thing if you are sitting in a comfortable movie theater watching a scary movie. But what do the firing of live machine guns and the bursting of mortar rounds do to the psyche of a five-year-old child? What kind of effect does the loss of security and stability have on a child who only knows constant turmoil, literally being pulled from one village to another and from one refugee camp to another out of fear for her family's lives?

This is a story about betrayal—the betrayal of national leaders, the betrayal of family members and the betrayal of self. And it is a story about loss—the loss of a beloved father, the temporary loss of a mother, the loss of identity and the loss of morality. But it is also a story of recovery and restoration. In one of the saddest stories, Lakhina tells how her mother abandoned her and her younger brother to the care of their grandparents as they were preparing to leave Thailand and immigrate to America. Also, one of the happiest stories tells about how, twenty-five years later, Lakhina, her mother, and her extended family were reunited.

Ultimately, this is a story about rebellion—rebellion from the expectations of family, rebellion from the sincere warnings of caring friends and rebellion against the numerous attempts of God to protect Lakhina from a corrupt society and from herself. And on the other hand, it is a story about submission—submission to God that led to a miraculous, life-changing experience, and submission to the unconditional love of her husband and his parents.

This is not only a story about Lakhina's physical journey through life but her spiritual journey as well. As a child in a Buddhist home, she had no concept of a loving God who was personally interested in her. However, as she grew older, her experiences in life, including the many miraculous times she and her family were saved from the grip of death, eventually paved the way for her to discover and accept the existence of a good God and His gift of salvation.

The horrors of the Killing Fields make this story an extraordinary one. However, it is, in many ways, just like ours. For no matter where we were born or how our family life may have been, the truth is this: every one of us has to eventually face and find answers to the great questions of life. And while few of us have ever experienced perils as traumatic as Lakhina's, all of us are on our own particular journey through the various fields of life. Hopefully yours, like Lakhina's, will take you through God's fields of grace into His loving arms.

Rev. Steven R. Brown
South Carolina District Superintendent
Assemblies of God

ACKNOWLEDGMENTS

*T*imothy, you are far greater and more handsome than the prince from the fairy-tale pages that I dreamed about as a little girl. Through you, I know what it is to be loved and to be cherished above rubies. You've won my heart. I will follow you anywhere, my prince!

Jaidon and Micah, you are our most precious gifts from God Almighty. You are here because mommy cried out in anguish during her time of desperation for God to reveal the width, the height and the depth of His infinite love for her. My sons, you are treasured gifts to my life. Through your sweet existence, my little cherubs, mommy has known true love!

Sopheak, thank you for giving me a tangible reason for drawing my next breath when life was wretchedly unbearable. It was you, my faithful brother, who pointed me to the God of hope. You were right, "If God can use Joyce Meyer's pain, God can use Lakhina's!" In that dark hour, those words you spoke gave me back my life. There will always be an extra-special spot reserved just for you inside my heart!

Mom and Dad Dittmer, thank you for the selfless sacrifices that you made in sharing your life with me and loving an enraged, unruly teenager. Where would I be today without your love? I will never cease to give God praise for bringing you both into my life!

Mom and Dad Brown, thank you for being such wonderful in-laws, for lavishing love on me and for making me feel so priceless. Thank you for your undying support of all that we are. What a great honor to be your daughter-in-law!

Pastors Terry and Anita Mahan, thank you for speaking life, hope, purpose and destiny into my life. Because of your proclamation of God's awesome destiny for His children, I am now living His life, pursuing all that He is in me!

Our greatest treasures in life are our countless wonderful friends here in Florida and around the globe. Because of you all, Tim, Jaidon, Micah and I are richly blessed beyond description. Thank you for your faithful love and support. Your friendship is God's promise of abundant life for our family. Thank you for joining with us as catalysts to advance our Father's glorious kingdom!

A special thanks to my wonderful father-in-law, Steven Brown, my precious friends Matt and Mary King, and "Nana Jean" for all the time and energy invested to make this momentous project possible!

INTRODUCTION

As a child, I often asked these haunting questions: Who am I? Why was I born? Where do I belong? Isn't there more to life than pain, misery and suffering? Will I ever find the true love that my heart is yearning for? Could someone ever love me unconditionally? Is there really a God?

At some point in your life, I'm sure you have pondered these questions. The question I present to you is this: have you found your answers? My prayer is that my story will help direct you to the God who holds the answers to our deepest questions. Actually, He does more than hold these answers—He is the answer! Being our Creator, He gave us inquisitive minds with deep, unanswered questions to cause us to seek Him. The Creator of the universe longs for us to know Him intimately.

I dedicate this book to the underdogs, the outcasts, the abandoned, the addicts, and the orphan-hearts of the world. Perhaps you are blessed and do not fit into one of these categories, but you may know someone who is struggling to find their place, purpose, and value in this world. It is my utmost desire that my personal triumphs over tragedy, written within these pages, will offer encouragement to those who are wounded from the traumas of life. I pray that God's undeniable goodness throughout each chapter will ignite hope in the heart of one who may feel hopeless.

Come journey through the shattered life of a little orphan refugee girl marked for death. From the Killing Fields of Cambodia through fields of betrayal, abduction, addictions and promiscuity, you will witness how God transformed those dark places into bright light, exposing His awesome love—a love so vast, so deep, and so high that it is almost incomprehensible. He is the true Author of *Through Fields of Grace* because He is the Author of my life! "For in him we live and move and have our being...We are his offspring" (Acts 17:28).

You can stop searching! Embrace the miracle worker who transformed me from death into life as your own personal Lord, Savior, Father, Friend and Lover of your heart and soul. He is the One who your heart has been longing for. He wants to give you peace beyond measure, joy uncontainable, and love everlasting! Are you ready to live?

"...For the Lord God is your life..." (Deuteronomy 30:20).

CHAPTER ONE

THE GREAT FALL

According to my mother in 1972 our little family was flourishing happily. My mother was pregnant with me and my newlywed parents were anxiously awaiting my arrival. With father as the Regiment Troop Commander in the Cambodian Military, life was good with a promising future ahead. In preparation for my birth, my father built a home for Mother to nest her soon to be born infant. She said it wasn't very big, but it was a pretty little house; a place that she loved.

I was born in Battambang, Cambodia, October of 1972, the Year of the Rat. Mother described me as a round and plump baby. I guess you could say that I was well-nourished!

Growing up as a child, I was mesmerized by daddy's contagious presence. He was nurturing and tender toward me. He loved to have fun, loved to sing, and loved to play his flute and banjo. Daddy was full of life! He always made opportunities to make me laugh. Although I remember so little about my father, he was indeed my world! He was my protector. One of my fondest memories of him was when he came running to rescue me from a severe lightning storm. When the lightning bolt struck nearby, I was petrified. Frozen by fear, I stood still screaming at the top of my lungs. Then suddenly, daddy was there lifting me into his strong, loving arms and carrying me inside our house. It was also daddy who taught me how to rub my feet together to remove the dust before climbing into bed. I was, like any typical daddy's girl, captivated by my flawless hero!

My daddy's older brother, Uncle Roeun, served alongside him in the Cambodian military. He told me of a fierce struggle where daddy prevailed, single-handedly over nearly a dozen Vietnamese soldiers. By the look on my uncle's face and his intense body language, I could tell that he was particularly proud of his brother. He told me that daddy wasn't afraid of anyone. Daddy was popular throughout the area and was known as a fierce hero for his battle victories. Men feared him and women loved him.

I guess that is why it was so hard for me to understand and believe what my mother told me about him could be true. It just seemed inconceivable that my daddy could do anything wrong. I remember wanting to argue with her, telling her she was mistaken and what she was telling me about my childhood hero couldn't be true.

One year after my birth, our family's promising future came to a shameful end. The generational curse that had destroyed our ancestors had returned to rob everything that was precious to our family's name. Like his father and grandfather, daddy's addiction had escalated to a shattering momentum that was too powerful for him to control. Mother admitted that she was ashamed of the fall of our family. What she told me I knew had to be true, but I did not want to accept it. I had wished that it was just a bad dream, but it wasn't. It was a very ugly, startling reality. And it was about my perfect hero!

The evil shame that brought the fall of our family's glory was my wonderful father's bondage to an insatiable addiction. He was enslaved to the destructive, compulsive behavior of gambling, and it eventually robbed us of everything. As daddy continued to feed his unquenchable passion for each wager, mother wept in shame. Time after time, she pleaded with him, "Please stop this madness before we lose everything!" But it was to no avail. Daddy's addiction drove him beyond his conscience's limits.

In the end, mother watched as daddy's debtors came in the middle of the night to collect their gambling prizes. They came at night in hopes of "saving face" for daddy so he would not lose the honor and respect of his neighbors. They hauled all of the furniture out, including the very bed that mother slept on. The embarrassment of this hideous curse stripped our family of all dignity, but unfortunately, it did not end there. After the money was gone and the furniture was collected, it finally came to a painful end. Mother's worst fear came true. Driven beyond reason, with one unfortunate roll of the dice, daddy gambled again and lost our home. Heart broken and humiliated, my family had to relinquish our home and begin looking for some other place of shelter.

Seeing what he had done and mother engulfed in such deep emotional pain, I know my daddy knew he needed to stop gambling. I am sure he tried to stop again and again, but obviously lacked the will power to overcome the addiction that had him so bound. At that point, no one had been able to explain to him about Jesus' redeeming blood that was shed to free him from his addictive curse. And because he had not heard this good news, he continued helplessly and totally consumed by his addictions.

"Do not be a man who strikes hands in pledge or puts up security for debts; if you lack the means to pay, your very bed will be snatched from under you"
(Proverbs 22:26).

Not long after we lost our home, mother gave birth to my younger brother, Sopheak. Sopheak was born in 1973, the Year of the Ox. Since there were no birth certificates issued in Cambodia, these ancient oriental calendar zodiacs actually played an important role in identifying our true ages.

Needless to say, times were hard when Sopheak was born. We had become wanderers, migrating with daddy from one patrol station to another. Because of daddy's military position, we were always on the move. Mother said that the only possessions we had were the clothes on our backs and a few pots and pans. Food was extremely scarce, so much so that it was often difficult for mother to produce the needed breast milk to feed my little brother. For about two years we bounced around from one station to the next with daddy.

On April 17, 1975, Cambodia entered a crossroad that would forever alter the course of the entire nation. It was New Year's week, the jolliest time of the year. The nation's men, women, boys and girls were all filled with cheery hearts anticipating the week-long festivity. Women were merrily preparing delicious meals and desserts to take to the monks at the temple. Young men and women were dressed in their best attire in hopes of attracting the opposite sex for possible marriage. Children were intoxicated with fun, playing traditional Cambodian New Year's games.

The bands were playing the Rourm Woung's traditional beats under the shady trees. Classical dancers, adorned in special costumes, performed royal dances and blessed the people with peace and prosperity for the coming year. People of all ages were proceeding to the nearest temple to present their offerings to Buddha for a better new year. The air was filled with the sounds of traditional music piped through the loud speakers, encouraging the spirit of celebration. Street vendors, with eager expectation, hoped for their biggest profit of the year selling food and goods.

While the young and old were sharing wishes of blessing and prosperity with one another, death was lurking in the shadow to end their New Year merriment without a warning. Suddenly, as the Khmer Rouge (Red Cambodians) discharged truck-loads of armed guerilla soldiers with AK-47s and machine guns, the scene of children's laughter turned into confusion and chaos. As tanks began rolling through the streets, broadcasting their poisonous propaganda, people ran wildly everywhere screaming and searching for their loved ones. The Khmer Rouge soldiers, many scarcely more than children themselves, were armed and ready to execute indiscriminately.

The command from the megaphone was for all to leave their homes and move out to the country right away. The lie told by the Khmer Rouge was that the United States was planning an attack on the nation's capital city, Phnom Penh, in three days. The soldiers commanded that the townspeople pack light and take only the bare necessities. They promised that the evacuation would only be a temporary move and that the people could return to their homes within a few days. Those who refused to leave their homes were dealt with immediately, through means of execution.

The New Year scenes that were once filled with gladness and celebration were abruptly replaced with fear and madness. The Khmer Rouge had begun their systematic execution of every doctor, lawyer, government official, teacher, and student, including people whose only crime was their need to wear glasses. Their diabolical philosophy was simple: annihilate every citizen with any semblance of education, prestige, or power. Intelligence represented a threat to the new mindless culture Pol Pot envisioned for Cambodia.

For Pol Pot's plan to succeed there had to be a national cleansing. For the new Cambodia to take root and grow, the old Cambodia had to be destroyed. The new Cambodia would consist of uneducated, lower class farmers. History remembers this evil conspiracy as The Killing Fields—a one-of-a-kind atrocity against millions of innocent human beings. It was nothing less than a horrendous bloodbath defying all human comprehension.

The Khmer Rouge, like heartless savages, would line up entire families and perform mass executions in broad day light. Their strategy was to instill a deep seated fear in the hearts of anyone who may be tempted to entertain any thoughts about rebelling against their authority. They were ready to kill, without hesitation, anyone that posed a threat to their bloody goals.

It was Pol Pot's goal to turn Cambodia into a Communist nation where only the powerful, like him, would benefit. His plan was to overthrow the reigning Prince Sihanouk Norodom. The Khmer Rouge taught that a new Cambodia was needed because the foundation of the old Cambodia was made up of a class of corrupted, gluttonous aristocrats who deserved death. They brainwashed their young soldiers with lies and propaganda to instill deep hate towards the middle and upper class Cambodians.

Pol Pot successfully established his tyrannical reign by winning the support of uneducated lower class masses from remote villages and wilderness areas. He knew they would be easy targets, open to brainwashing, because they had nothing to lose but everything to gain. He enticed them with promises of power, control, and better living conditions. He persuaded them that loyalty to his revolution would mean an abundance of food and guaranteed positions for their future.

Pol Pot played on the hatred of those who already harbored jealousy and resentment toward the prosperous city people. It was carefully sowed seeds of selfishness and greed that formed the ultimate madness that spawned the Killing Fields. God's Word says, "For where you have envy and selfish ambition, there you find disorder and every evil practice" (James 3:16). How else can one explain the demonic-like brutality waged against millions of innocent Cambodians?

Pol Pot unleashed his execution squads with a permit to capture and kill. People like my father, a trained military warrior, posed the greatest threat of all to their new terrorist government. From the beginning of their reign in April 1975, death warrants surfaced all over the nation, demanding the innocent lives of all government officials and professionals of all trades. Father's position elevated him to the top of the Khmer Rouge's execution list, so the search was on for daddy and for my family.

For the four years following 1975, our family and countless others became fugitives. We fled from one town to the next, from village to village, changing our names and hiding our true identities from our captors. Mother buried every picture of father and destroyed every piece of evidence that would link him to the military and to us. Unfortunately, the Khmer Rouge had already ransacked his patrol station and taken the picture of him that was hanging on his office wall in Battambang. That picture was all the proof the Khmer Rogue needed of his connection to the Cambodian militia. And so, it seemed that his fate would soon be sealed by death itself.

We rarely stayed in any one place more than two to three months. Eventually whispers would begin circulating between the townspeople, warning us that our enemy was close. Then as soon as night would fall, we would gather our few belongings and hit the road once more. We were like thieves who vanished in the darkness of night seeking refuge in another nearby village or town. Because of daddy's well-known reputation, he knew that there was really no safe place anywhere for him to hide. He knew that regardless of where he went, people would recognize him. His high profile fugitive status kept us distant from the rest of our other families. They were afraid that we would bring them harm and jeopardize their lives.

One night, father sneaked out with Sopheak to grandmother's house at a different village. After he arrived he told his mother about his fear of being captured. He knew, with two small children and a pregnant wife, that he would not be able to outrun his enemies for long. Evidently, it was at that time that daddy's younger brother urged him to flee to Thailand for safety. He argued that it was daddy's only chance of escaping the Khmer Rouge alive. But daddy did not have the heart to leave us, especially mother. She was due to give birth any day. He refused to leave his beloved wife and two young children behind in order to save his own life.

In their secret meeting, Daddy desperately shared his heart's wish with his mother, pleading with her to take care of his children after he was gone. He told her, "Mother, there's no way that I can hide from them forever. They will find me and they will kill me. I am worried about my children. My wife is still very young and beautiful. One day she will be married to another man. But I am afraid that her new husband will mistreat my children. Promise me that you will take care of them after I'm gone. Promise me that you will do this for me, so that I may die in peace!"

Out of her deep love and compassion for her son, Grandma agreed to his last request. Daddy's younger sister, who heard their conversation, later told me that they embraced and cried together that heartbreaking night, clinging to one another knowing it could very well be their last farewells.

Not long after that mother gave birth to another baby boy, who father named Bountho after his honored General who was slain by the Khmer Rouge. The very week of Bountho's birth, father wanted to build Sopheak and me a wooden swing. I remember crossing the street from our home carrying our tools. Since I was the oldest, I was appointed to be daddy's little helper. While he was up in the tree, he would need my assistance. With great pride and a joyful grin, I would hand him more nails. I was already anticipating the great fun-filled rides that we would soon be enjoying. My little heart was bursting with gratitude for daddy's kindness.

But before our exciting little project was complete, I noticed a white car approaching from the distance. As the car came closer, something seemed wrong and I began to feel that this was not a good thing. When it finally reached us, four men, all dressed in black, got out of a white convertible. Immediately, my once joyful heart was filled with dread.

Then one of the men asked daddy to come down from the tree and verify his name. When he reached the ground I ran to him and grabbed on to one of his legs. I began to cry hysterically. One of the men, trying to calm me down, told me everything would be alright. He said that they were not going to hurt my daddy. However, in my young mind I somehow knew that those men meant him harm rather than good. In my desperation, I began pleading with them for mercy: "Please, don't take my daddy away from me!" "Please, sirs, don't take my daddy!"

I remember begging daddy, while clinging tightly to his legs, "Pa, please don't go with them!" While I knew somehow daddy really didn't have any choice, I had hoped my pleas would somehow make a difference. The men told me that they were going to take him to a celebration of some sort. But deep down inside, I knew that they were lying to me. Daddy told me, "Don't worry, its okay. Don't cry, my child. Go home and tell mother that they have taken me!"

After daddy pried my arms off his leg, I stood there helplessly, watching them put him into the car. I remember as the white car drove off down the dusty road with my hero inside. Then and there, I knew that I would never see my daddy again. I wanted to die that day, but I couldn't. Because I was daddy's helper and he told me to go home and tell mother about his capture. When I did, she let out a scream that pierced the very core of my being. It wasn't long before we all began a chorus of heart-rending cries, holding each other tightly while mourning our missing protector.

Although I cannot recall ever seeing father again after that dreadful day, mother told me that on that particular day, the Khmer Rouge only took him for interrogation. While the plot against him was not over, he was eventually released. The Khmer Rouge tried to mislead him by telling him that the orders to execute military officers had been rescinded. They tried to convince him that Pol Pot only desired peace, and that the killing had ended. They baited him with the false hope that Cambodia would once again be united and believing this, he had no reason to withhold his true identity. They promised him that he would not be put to death or in any way punished for telling them the truth.

Mother told me how weary daddy was of being on the run and how tired he became of living a life of lies. He wanted so desperately to believe that he was no longer in danger. With this conviction, Mother told me that daddy surrendered to his enemies and told them the truth of his identity; that he had been a commanding officer for the Cambodian military. After his release, daddy returned home to tell mother the great news that Cambodia was once again at peace and that he was no longer wanted by the Khmer Rouge. He assured her that his enemy had granted him freedom and his life. But she was terrified by what he told her. Mother's heart plunged into despair. She told me how she sobbed bitterly because he had fallen for their lies. She shouted at him, "What have you done? They've lied to you. The country is not at peace. Your confession has signed your death warrant!"

No doubt! My family desperately needed to flee from the Khmer Rouge that night, but because mother had so recently given birth to Bountho, she was not able to make such a treacherous trip. Three days after daddy's confession to the Khmer Rouge, Daddy disappeared and never came home.

In desperation, she approached the Khmer Rouge village ruler and begged him to tell her what had become of her husband. He only told her lies trying to comfort her. He said, "Oh, we have chosen a few strong men to cut down a bamboo forest some distance from here. Your husband is with them. Don't worry about him; the work will only take a few days. He will be back soon!"

Mother replied, "You are lying to me. Tell me the truth! You have killed my husband and he will never come home. You have killed him, haven't you? Please don't lie to me, just tell me the truth!" Day after day she pled with them to tell her what had happened to the love of her life. But all she got from them were more lies to cover up the horrid truth.

Later mother learned from her neighbors that they had seen my daddy. He was tied up in the back of a truck along with other prisoners. They said the Khmer Rouge's truck broke down in front of our very home. It took the soldiers almost twenty minutes to fix the problem less than fifty feet from mother's view. Because daddy knew where mother was lying, he did not dare look in her direction.

Fortunately, she was distracted by neighbors who had come in to see the newborn baby. Some of them saw what was taking place and deliberately blocked mother's view so that she would not be able to see daddy's forlorn face inside the truck. They were afraid that she would be unable to take such trauma because she was still weak from childbirth.

Later, when Mother narrated this tragic event to me, I asked her, "What would you have done if you had seen daddy in the truck that day?" Without hesitation, she exclaimed, "I would have run after him!" It was obvious, by the passion of her response that she had been very much in love with my daddy and nothing could have kept her away from him. Within that moment, I sensed that God was whispering to me that it was by His mercy and grace that mother's eyes were kept hidden from the heartbreak of that tragic day. By blocking her view, God shielded us and preserved our lives from our enemies. If she would have seen daddy bound in the back of that truck, she would have run to him. There is no doubt then, that the Khmer Rouge would have finished our family off along with my father at that critical moment.

> *"He will cover you with his feathers, and under his wings you will find refuge; his faithfulness will be your shield and rampart"*
> (Psalm 91:4).

CHAPTER TWO

THROUGH THE KILLING FIELDS

With daddy captured, we knew that it would only be a matter of time before our executioners would return to exterminate the rest of our family. The Khmer Rouge's order was to eliminate every last person sharing the same bloodline as their enemies. Mother waited till nightfall to put her plans into action. As darkness fell, mother gathered all three of us children and fled from our home. Once again, we disappeared into the black night as fugitives on the run.

We walked all night and on into the next day until we came to a horrible stench. The offensive odor was not something familiar to me. The further we went the more disgusting the horrible stench became. No matter which way we turned our heads, there was no escape. I soon learned that it was the stench of decaying bodies rotting in the hot sun.

My curiosity overcame my disdain for the smell. I wanted to see who these dead people were so I speedily ran ahead to take a closer look. As I focused my eyes on the dead woman's face, I let out a startling shout, "Mak! It's Auntie, our next door neighbor, and her two babies!" Quickly, my mind raced back to the last time I had seen her alive. I remembered how forlorn she looked as she went inside her house and closed the door.

Like us, the Khmer Rouge had just taken her husband. As I stood gazing at that horrible scene, I realized those could have just as well been our bodies lying there in the hot sun. Instinctively, I knew that if we didn't keep on moving this would be our chilling fate as well. I could see tears welling up in mother's eyes as she struggled not to vomit after witnessing her friend and babies mercilessly slaughtered in the open fields like worthless beasts.

Because the entire nation was under the control and watchful eyes of the Khmer Rouge, it seemed like escape would be impossible. Soon we found ourselves at a new village under the supervision of a new Khmer Rouge leader. His primary responsibility was to supervise over seventy widows and their children. Like my mother, many of these widows had lost their husbands to the hands of these cold-blooded killers. Fortunately for us, my beautiful young mother found favor with the leader in our new village.

Instead of being stuffed into overcrowded shacks along with the other seventy broken families, we were invited to live with him. Mother said he was a very nice man with a gentle nature. Regardless, living with him resulted in better food and much better living conditions than the other families. Because of his tenderness toward my lovely young mother, her labor assignment was also much lighter than the others. Although technically, at the age of five, I satisfied the Khmer Rouge's work standards, I was not forced to go out to work with the other children. I was granted the privilege of staying at home to care for my two little brothers.

Our privileged situation, however, soon became the center of a village uprising. Because of the favors and special treatment that we'd received from the kind Khmer Rouge camp leader, words of jealousy and envy broke out in the camp. Our fellow villagers brought accusations against the camp leader and my mother. The so-called crime they were guilty of was love and compassion. They were falsely accused of having an affair. The penalty for this type of crime, under the new tyrannical government, was disembowelment. Once again, our welfare was threatened because of vicious lies and rumors. Mother later assured me that there was never any type of love affair between them; just compassion from a caring

Khmer Rouge leader who cared deeply for her. The accusers could not build a case against them because it was not true.

> *"You shall hide them in the secret place of your presence from the plots of man; you shall keep them secretly in a pavilion from the strife of tongues"*
> (Psalm 31:20, NKJV).

Mother believed that we were safe because of the Khmer Rouge leader's graciousness toward us. However, now, I totally believe that it was God's mercy that gave us favor. It was God who caused our camp leader to look upon us with tenderness and compassion. And it was God who actually lavished His love and mercy on us through that camp leader. God's love, through him, shielded us. As mother shared this story, I began to realize that twenty-five years ago, before I ever knew about God, He was already causing our enemies to be at peace with us. God used an enemy, the kind Khmer Rouge ruler, to look after us and to care for us; giving favor to my beautiful mother. How God did this simply confounds my mind!

> *"You prepare a table before me in the presence of my enemies. You anoint my head with oil; my cup overflows"*
> (Psalm 23:5).

Even though we had favor, the grim reality is that life was still very difficult. Mother had to leave us early every morning, before the sun came up, and wouldn't return until sundown every evening. I can still remember those frightfully long days of being left alone with my two younger brothers. Sopheak was almost four at the time and Bountho was about a year old. During the day, the village was like a ghost town, with everyone gone to their assigned duties.

It was winter and I can still remember how bitterly cold it became when the wind blew. To keep warm, Sopheak and I would actually sit in the middle of the road to try to warm ourselves in the bright sunlight. Sometimes, when I got hungry, I stole food from our next door neighbor. I guess you could describe me as a nosey child because I watched closely where our neighbors hid their food. I must have also been an inept thief, however, because our neighbors always seemed to know that I was the one who stole their hidden food.

During the long days, I can remember Sopheak and me chasing frogs, crickets and dragonflies for entertainment. Or sometimes we watched crabs swimming in a nearby pond. When it rained hard, the little ponds would flood leaving a couple of feet of water above the pool's edge. I remember walking in the water once and mother having to pull three or four leeches off my ankle. That was a terrifying experience. To this day, my memory of those black bloodsucking creatures is still beyond revolting.

When it comes to my baby brother, Bountho, I still find it painful to admit how little I remember taking care of him. One of the few memories I have of him was hearing him screaming frantically. Disturbed by his desperate cry, Sopheak and I both ran inside to check on him. We saw him squirming in his hammock bed in his own urine and feces. To our shock, we watched him ingesting his own feces. We found it so repulsive that we ran off, leaving our baby brother alone.

Later that evening, after her long day of toiling in the fields, mother returned home. We were thrilled to see her, but her attention quickly turned to her baby. Within moments after checking on him, mother let out the most gut-wrenching scream I have ever heard. I wondered what would cause my mother to scream out like that.

Her screams brought the neighbors rushing over to our house. I did not understand all the crying and wailing that went on that night. Confused, I stayed out of the way and watched with Sopheak. I remembered wondering if someone had died and I hadn't been told. Why else would mother and our neighbors appear to be in such agonizing grief? I knew it was the cry of death because I'd heard that type of cry before!

That night fell and mother and the villagers were all walking along in a single line. I was walking next to mother and Sopheak. Some were playing, what to my young mind was gloomy music while others were carrying lanterns to light the way. I had no idea where we were going so late at night. My curious little mind was filled with questions, but no one seemed to notice. I was wondering what the two men were carrying on the wooden board on their shoulders. It looked like something small wrapped up in cloth. The procession moved on slowly with mother, still sobbing, holding tightly to our hands.

When we finally arrived at our destination, a couple of men brought out a shovel and began digging in the ground. After a while, they laid the small bundle of cloth in the hole and covered it up with dirt. Mother's cries became even louder. It seemed as though she was going to die as they buried that bundle. After the men were finished, we all marched back home. Mother was over come with utter grief and sorrow! From that time on, there never seemed to be a good time to ask any of my questions about that night.

It took me a few days to finally realize that I was no longer hearing Bountho's cry. Maybe he wasn't ever coming back to be with us again and that's why mother was so despondent. I don't believe I ever shed a tear over my little brother's death, as I did not understand death fully at that age.

In actuality, it wasn't until after I had returned home to Cambodia twenty-five years later that I somewhat realized the depth of mother's agony over my brother's death. As a child, I had never considered how every morning when mother was forced to leave her two small sons in the care of her six-year-old daughter, that the thing she feared most was coming home to discover her lifeless infant boy. But she had no choice in the matter. I am sure she understood that a six year old was neither mature enough nor experienced enough to give her baby the kind of supervision he needed.

She also knew that Bountho, without her, did not have the essential nourishment he needed. How hopelessly tormented she must have felt, knowing every moment while she was away that her little baby might die of starvation. Coming to this realization some twenty-five years later, I was able to mourn for my brother's death.

It wasn't until after I had returned from Cambodia, as I stood by watching my seven-month-old infant boy, Jaidon, helplessly squirming and crying in his crib because he was hungry, thoughts of baby Buntho crossed my mine. Like a heaving dam, my heart burst with grief and sorrow over the suffering of my deceased baby brother. Painful memories of him, screaming for someone to feed him flashed through my mind. Deep remorse filled my soul as I remembered that I was not able to provide for his basic needs!

Stricken with sorrow, I picked up my own son and squeezed him tightly, close to my chest. With tears streaming down my face, I gave voice my regret that it took me so long to realize and acknowledge Bountho's pain and suffering. I repented over the fact that I had never celebrated his life or mourned his death. I realized that for twenty-five years I had never truly acknowledged his existence. I was only six years old then so I just didn't have that many memories of him. But as a Christian, and now seeing life through the eyes of a mother, I accepted him and realized that his short life was indeed precious and significant to God and therefore, precious and significant to me.

I believe the tears I shed that day brought me much needed healing, a healing that I didn't even know I needed. Immediately I felt a sense of peace and closure and, for the first time in my life, somehow connected my spirit with my little brother's. Since that experience, it is with eager anticipation that I look forward to seeing him when I get to heaven. How delightful to know that Bountho is not only a part of my past, but he is also going to be a part of my future. One day we will be together throughout all eternity. What an awesome hope that I have in Jesus: one day Bountho and I will be reunited as brother and sister again in our Father's kingdom. It makes me smile to know that Bountho is with his heavenly Father and enjoying the riches of His kingdom, a place where there is no more lack. It is a place where there is no more hunger, no more pain, and no more suffering—but plenty of love!

Through that experience, I was able to understand why day after day, Sopheak and I watched mother leave for work in despair, and returned so run down and tormented. I remember how she would come home after sundown all covered with mud and dirt. Then she'd walk right pass us and crawl straight into her corner, where she'd sob heartbreakingly. After Bountho's death, she plunged into a deep depression. It seemed as though a part of her soul had died with him.

One evening as she was lying on the floor sobbing, I saw a caterpillar crawling on her muddy back. I screamed out to her, "Mak, you have a caterpillar on your back!" I was certain that she would scream and jump up to her feet to try to get the critter off her back. But to my bewilderment, she didn't even move. She just kept on sobbing! It was as though I was talking to the air. She was too distressed to even respond. I'd often wondered if we meant anything at all to her. It appeared to me that our own mother had become deaf, dumb and dead to us.

Night after night, we'd watch her cry until she had no more tears. Eventually she would simply fall asleep in exhaustion. She rarely spoke and seldom would eat anything. It appeared that she had little desire to keep on living. I am certain that if it hadn't been for Sopheak and me, her wish would have been to never wake from her sleep. How could a six year old fully understand the depth of a mother's pain and agony?

One sunny afternoon, I began eavesdropping on a private conversation between mother and some of our neighbors. They were whispering softly about what they had seen earlier that day. Being the nosey child that I was, I stood quietly outside of the curtain, listening as they shared their secrets.

Evidently the women had recently been forced to watch the execution of two people accused of expressing love for one another. They shared the terrible details of how the Khmer Rouge stripped both the man and the woman of all their clothing. Then they were tied in back of two horses and dragged naked across sharp, freshly cut bamboo stakes. They were dragged around like rag dolls until their bodies were cut to ribbons flinging their organs all over the fields.

Again, the Khmer Rouge was making an example of them to the rest of the villagers. Their message was clear: those who dared to show affection of any type toward the opposite sex would end up like them. How can I describe the horrible impression hearing all the chilling details made on me. All that kept going through my innocent mind was, "How could anyone be that wicked and heartless?" I just could not fathom mankind's brutality against one another.

It is hard to imagine how much wickedness mother saw under the terror reign of the Khmer Rouge. She told me that when it was time for mass executions, the Khmer Rouge would use loud speakers in order to drown out the screams of their victims during the bloodbath. Then they would heartlessly antagonize the remaining victims by parading, before them the clothing taken from their dead loved ones. But no one dared to shed a tear when the Khmer Rouge flaunted these gruesome garments. Paralyzed with fear, the terrorized group could only watch silently.

Mother recalled the many times when the Khmer Rouge would walk past her carrying the organs of their victims, their bloodshot eyes piercing into her very soul. That is where they got their name, "Khmer Rouge." "Khmer" means native Cambodians and "Rouge" is the French word for red, which stands for their Communist ideology and represents the blood that flowed in the Killing Fields.

Mother called the Khmer Rouge fierce predators because they supposedly ate the organs of their victims. It was as if they were not human! Rumors, like blood on the Killing Fields, flowed freely, suggesting that eating their victims' organs while they were still alive supposedly gave them supernatural power.

Young children and babies seemed to be choice delicacies for many of these fiendish demons. In my personal opinion, they were no more than demons in human flesh. No human being could ever commit such atrocities unless they were truly possessed by Satan himself. It was Satan, the father of destruction, who was behind the abhorrent butchery. The Khmer Rouge were Satan's children, influenced, possessed, and controlled by him to perpetrate his wicked plan upon God's precious creation.

"...You belong to your father, the devil, and you want to carry out your father's desire. He was a murderer from the beginning..."
(John 8:44).

The trauma that mother had endured under their reign of terror would explain her despondent moods and crying spells. Again and again I watched as she would show no interest in her daily bowl of porridge. It wasn't long before I became deeply concerned that she might die from starvation. I had to do something to keep from losing the most valuable treasure left in my life. The appalling thought of facing a world without her was out of the question. After all, how could a six year old with a younger brother to take care of make it if mother were to die? With an abundance of youthful imagination, it didn't take me long to come up with a plan to save her life.

Later that very day, I decided it was time to put my plan into action! She needed more than porridge; she needed meat! So Sopheak and I started out to steal two catfish from the local Khmer Rouge cafeteria. I thought that once mother ate the fish, she would be normal again.

It was the community mealtime and all the widow's children would go to the cafeteria to receive their small bowl of porridge. I remember that it was a rainy, dismal day. I told Sopheak to reach into one of the barrels where the live catfish were kept and hide one of the fish in his shirt. Then I would do the same. I warned my partner in crime that when his deed was done not to look back but to just keep running toward home. I specifically told him don't stop running regardless of what happened to me!

Sopheak was successful in his mission. He snatched a catfish out of the barrel, stuffed it up his shirt, and ran as fast as he could toward home. Quickly I followed my little brother's example. I reached into the barrel, grabbed a fish and slipped it under my shirt. Holding on to my slimy prize tightly I began to run toward the gate at the end of the barbed wire fence. With the pelting raindrops beating in my face and my heart beating fiercely against my chest, the thought of success energized me with each step.

Just as I thought I was in the clear, I heard, behind me, the stern command from a soldier, "Stop! Stop or I'll shoot!" The command was followed by the sound of the bolt on the AK-47 sliding a shell into the chamber. I knew that the soldier was ready to fire and I could almost imagine that bullet tearing into my back. Terrified, I stopped in my tracks and dropped the fish. Paralyzed by fear, I stood still, screaming from the top of my lungs. Petrified that my life was about to end, I urinated in my pants, drenched in the blaring thunder. Only this time, my hero was not around to come running to my rescue!

Shockingly, for some reason, the soldier did not shoot me. The penalty for stealing was torture and death. At the time, I had no idea that I had been miraculously delivered from the hands of my enemy. Looking back, I clearly see that it was truly God's remarkable intervention that snatched me from the grave that dreadful day.

Even though I did commit a crime against the Khmer Rouge, and stole from them, God moved on my behalf and gave me mercy instead of judgment for my crime. If The Khmer Rouge had shot me, they would only be fulfilling the law, since I did break the law. The penalty for theft was death, but because of God's profound love for me, he looked beyond my sin. He saved me from being condemned by my executioner.

> *"[It is the Lord] who redeems your life from the pit*
> *and crowns you with love and compassion"*
> (Psalm 103:4)

CHAPTER THREE

THROUGH VALLEYS OF DEATH

After Buntho's death, we moved to be with our grandmother, mother's mother. With two little children, it was impossible for mother to be free to hunt for our essentials. She couldn't bear watching us go hungry, but if she had stayed with us, we wouldn't have anything to eat. Defying the Communist policy, mother repeatedly broke their rigid law of obtaining means of survival other than the community meal they gave us twice a day.

The Communists did not allow civilians to own anything privately. We were not allowed to grow our own herb or vegetable gardens or to raise livestock; we couldn't even own a chicken egg. Every plant, animal and possession belonged to the Communist government. They decided what we ate and we were only allowed to eat what they gave us. It was usually a small bowl of porridge with a few spoonfuls of rice accompanying two grains of raw salt for flavoring. That was our generous daily meal.

Often during mother's break time, she would disappear in the vicinity of a nearby pond or creek. She would fashion a fishing pole from a stick in hopes of catching fish or she would forage for something else for us to eat. Sometimes she'd catch crabs, small shrimp, or even snails. For vegetables, she would dig up bamboo shoots, water chestnuts and edible leaves. If it wouldn't kill us, mother fed it to us!

The Khmer Rouge took notice that she was in defiance of their strict regulations. Again and again, they demanded that she stop her hunting habits because it went against their policy. They even threatened her with execution. But mother's brave retort was simply, "When you stop feeding your children, then I'll stop feeding mine!" Recently I asked her if she was afraid of them. Sarcastically, she remarked, "I was past the point of fear. I had lost so much already! I would rather have us all dead than to suffer starvation!" I believe her iron-like determination came from the fact that she had already lost one baby to starvation and she wasn't about to let that happen again—ever!

During our stay at grandmother's house, mother left us, not only to forage for food but also look for father around the nearby concentration camps. Her heart ached to find him. He was indeed her lost love. Of course, from my childish point of view, I couldn't understand how mother could even think about actually leaving us behind that way. I was appalled. She should have known how desperately we needed her. We cried our hearts out, pulling on her legs begging her, "Please Mak, don't go! Please don't leave us!"

But her determination was unwavering. Although every parting from mother was emotionally traumatizing, as time passed, spending times at grandmother's house wasn't so bad. It was actually quite a nice change from the daily exile from the rest of the world. I felt safe with my grandparents because I felt they could protect us. I wasn't left alone to fend for Sopheak and for myself without adult supervision.

While I don't have many memories of our stay at my grandparents, one particular day does stand out. It was a beautiful, bright sunny day. Sopheak and I were walking through grandma's sweet potato field enjoying the carefree day without any worries or cares. I remember running along the riverbank near grandma's house playing with my little brother. We watched grandmother's husband, our step-grandfather, set some home made fish and crab traps along the bank. I always enjoyed pulling out one of grandpa's barrel to see if there was anything in it.

Once we found a catfish. As we went to pull it out, the fish slipped out of our hands and flopped around on the grassy bank. All of us were trying to catch it but it kept slipping out of our hands. The fish kept jumping and flopping further and further away as we continued to chase after it along the river bank. It was as though that fish was walking on the bank. To this day, I think it must have been a walking catfish. Suddenly our fish chasing fun came to an abrupt end when we saw a military helmet floating down the stream. I stood still for a moment while my heart raced with intensity, wondering who was going to be following the trail of that floating helmet.

Sopheak and I sprinted toward the object of our curiosity. Just as I had frightfully discerned, there trailing behind the helmet was a decomposing corpse of a soldier floating down the river. Needless to say, we were startled! My heart went out for the poor dead man. Immediately, questions began flooding my mind: "I wonder who he was? Where did he come from? Who were his mother and father? Was he married? Did he have any children?" Then I started thinking about my father. Had he, like this poor soldier, been killed? Was my precious hero dead: abandoned somewhere like the wretched man floating there in front of my eyes?

Well, after three brutal years as fugitives our pursuers finally caught up with us. Somehow, the Khmer Rouge discovered our identities and our relationship to daddy. Once again the grave was calling our names and death was perched, ready to swallow us once and for all. The Khmer Rouge was hellish, like fiends with a seething thirst for blood; something that my father's life alone could not quench. Their orders were to obliterate our family line from the face of the earth. Their ultimate goal was to destroy the tree along with its roots and seeds.

One hazy evening, mother, Sopheak, and I, along with about fifteen other families were rounded up and herded to a meeting. We were told that we were being relocated to a new village. But mother knew that relocation was the Khmer Rouge's code word for execution. She had seen their deceptive tactics at work too many times before.

Not wanting to be left behind, Grandma pleaded for the Khmer Rouge to allow her to go with us so she could help mother on this journey. Sopheak and I were small and Grandma saw that it would be grueling for a single mother to care for both of us by herself. At first, the Khmer Rouge showed no mercy, but she was persistence and did not give up. Grandma also sensed that we were being led to the slaughter. And as a widow herself, she had no desire to live without us. After repeated requests, the Khmer Rouge finally gave in and granted her permission to join us.

The following day, the Khmer Rouge came and gathered fifteen families that were on their list. There were at least seventy people in all, from babies to the elderly. Everyone was told to pack lightly. We were only allowed to take the clothes we were wearing along with a couple pots and pans and a little bit of rice, our group began the journey toward the valley of death.

After walking for hours, evening finally settled in around us. We were all physically drained and terribly hungry. The Khmer Rouge ordered us to set up camp in the midst of a desolate field. They told the women to start a fire and cook some rice for the famished group. The troop spread out in the field and began to settle in for the night while the women prepared, what could well be our last meal. After we ate, we were ordered to go to sleep to prepare for the next day's early morning journey. Like good little lambs, every family, with the exception of two, submitted to the Khmer Rouge's demands.

Mother and grandma decided that since we would all likely be dead by daybreak, they both felt it would be better to try to escape than to simply do nothing. The truth was, and they both knew it, we would face a torturous death if caught. They would make examples of us showing the others what happens to those who dare rebel against them.

That night the sky was pitch black with no lights other than the stars and the moon to guide our way. Once again, to our advantage, the Khmer Rouge did not have any flashlights. It was a prime opportunity to sneak off into the darkness without being seen. Mother sensed that it was now or never. Although both she and grandma were frightened, the chance for us to live far outweighed their fear of death.

Quickly and quietly, while the others were lying down to rest, grandma took my hand, while mother picked up my little brother. They quickly carried us off into the darkness. Within, what seemed like only seconds, we disappeared into the nearby woods. Almost immediately after we left the edge of the field, mother's worst nightmare came true. The Khmer Rouge discovered that we were missing. They realized this after doing an evening roll call. Indeed, there were two missing families unaccounted for.

Mother said she could hear them shouting amidst the camp: "Two families are missing! Two families have run off. We must find them!" Evidently, there was another brave family that night that shared our daring idea and made the same brave effort to escape. Mother told me that at that moment, she was horrified beyond belief! She thought, this time, for sure, our date with death had come.

We were at the point of no return. It was the moment of great truth. If we died that night, it would forever end daddy's lineage. To mother, it seemed almost certain that we would be caught since the sounds of our enemies' shouts were so close behind. But she and grandma did not surrender to their fears. Their strong drive to survive pushed them blindly forward into the black night. We hid in bushes and just kept on scurrying forward from bush to bush and from field to field until sunrise.

After their fruitless search, the Khmer Rouge evidently gave up and returned to the camp. Ironically, the next day we came across that other family. Excitedly, mother greeted them, "Oh, you ran, too? They were searching for you too!" Ecstatically, both families shared their joyful victory, having, for at least the time being, both cheated death. As for the other thirteen families, mother mourned for their malicious fate in the killing fields. She was certain that death had swallowed them.

> *"Like sheep they are destined for the grave,*
> *and death will feed on them.*
> *But God will redeem my life from the grave;*
> *he will surely take me to himself"*
> (Psalm 49:14-15).

I tremble every time I think of how God spared my family that night. I cannot grasp the reason why He would choose to show us mercy when we were no better than those other families? I suppose I will never understand God's unlimited mercy and grace upon my life. I am in awe and filled with gratitude for His never failing goodness. It is clear to me that it was God who hid my family that night. We were safe under the blanket of night and the shadow of the Almighty for our covering.

> *"For in the time of trouble He shall hide me in His pavilion;*
> *in the secret place of His tabernacle He shall hide me;*
> *He shall set me high upon a rock"*
> (Psalm 27:5, NKJV).

Naturally, we never went back to that village. I don't remember exactly where my step-grandfather went or what happened to him? But as for mother, grandmother, Sopheak and me, we went on to be with some of our other relatives. Given that we were fugitives, most of our relatives were afraid to take us in. Sadly, many of our own families even refused to hide father since he was such a high profile fugitive. Obviously, they did not want to risk their own lives and the lives of their children. Fortunately for us many of my aunts and uncles did extend mercy to us. This time we stayed in a little village with my father's mother and his siblings, while mother left once more in search for food.

Within weeks, our peaceful solitude was disrupted. We were once again attacked in the middle of the night. Fortunately, at the time of the assault, mother had just returned. Having her there meant the world to me. It brought much needed comfort to my distressed soul. It helped me to cope with the shock of war. Mother grabbed me with one hand and Sopheak with the other as we fled. I could feel the concussion of the exploding grenades and the zing of searching bullets. Once again, our safe haven had become another bloodbath, a scene that I had experienced much too often. The grave was once again screaming out for our very lives.

Initially, we ran, along with some other families and neighbors, down inside a large trench-like hole. I can still vividly remember the explosions thundering around us. I was terrified. All I could think about was, "What if the Khmer Rouge finds us in here? All they'd have to do is throw a grenade in here and we would all be killed in an instant. There would be no chance of escape." The very place that was supposed to offer us protection could turn out to be our collective grave. I guess the adults who were hiding in that trench with me must have had similar thoughts, because we didn't stay there very long. I remember us all running out of the trench like frantic mice toward the closest field for refuge.

There were possibly two to three families who flocked to the same banana field with us that night. We all had one goal in mind: to seek shelter from our pursuers. The night was dark and chilly. Fearfully, we waited in utter silence wondering whether we would escape or if our enemy would find us and slaughter us. In the distance we watched our little village being destroyed as the Khmer Rouge fire burned it to the ground. I could still hear the thundering blast of the grenades.

In the midst of my terror, I recall gazing up into the sky where I noticed, jutting out from the dark canopy of night, twinkling stars and a glowing moon. Exhausted, I slumped to the ground to try to rest my weary body. As I lay there looking up through the banana leaves the brightness of the stars and the moon beaming above somehow brought comfort and relief to my traumatized soul. They became beams of hope in my troubled heart. It seemed as though their glow was reassuring me that light shines most brightly where there is utter darkness. I have no doubt that it was my heavenly Father's way of comforting me. He was sending me a message of hope as if to say personally to me, that as long as there are bright stars and a shining moon somewhere in the sky, there will never be complete darkness. I know that it was my Heavenly Father who took time to minister to my heart that dark night telling me, "Hang on, there is still hope!"

We continued on our journey toward a little village in Tmarh Khole, where two of my mother's sisters lived. And as she had done so many times before, soon after our arrival at the village mother vanished once again. I missed her and frequently wept over her disappearance, wishing that she would come back.

I do recall some sweet memories living with my Auntie Leang and Auntie Laang. I remember having such fun each day as we visit the rice fields with our older cousin, Nee, who was only five years older than me. Sopheak and I would follow her around the emerald green rice paddies to hunt for food. We'd catch frogs, fish, and even shrimp. We learned how to find fresh water chestnuts and dig them out from the moist ground. The tastiest sautéed shrimp I ever had were the shrimp we caught during those short but happy days.

Even though we all worked hard to catch them, we only got to eat a tiny portion of them. The rest of the shrimp were taken from us by another relative who decided that she would feed her own children with our catch instead. There was nothing that we could do. Mother wasn't there to fend for us. And none of the other relatives came to our aid for fear of a confrontation. Later, mother returned. I remember that she brought back three bags of rice and some other goodies.

Shortly after her return, I was playing with the neighborhood children in our backyard. We were having an amusing time dancing, singing, and making flutes and horses out of banana branches and leaves. All of a sudden, while enjoying our games, I stepped on a scorpion. I will never forget the hellish stinging pain. I let out such an excruciating scream I think everyone in the village heard me. The pain was so bad that I couldn't stand so I fell to the ground and waited for mother to come to my rescue.

She came running to me, scooped me up into her arms and ran into the house. When she realized how serious my situation was she raced out looking for the village doctor. The witch doctor performed some "healing" ritual on me. The lady was aggressive; singing, dancing, and calling out to her ancestors and the spirits. I was terrified by her presence. Then she sprinkled some special kind of water on me and burned me with incense forming a triangle around my navel. Then she forced me to drink fresh coconut juice with some kind of black worm swimming in it. Horrified by the slimy worm wiggling in my juice, I kicked and screamed so hard you would have thought they were preparing to cut my throat. They prevailed, however, forcing the juice with the worm down my throat.

I don't remember what happened after that, except the ritual didn't help me very much. My temperature increased and I was feverishly sick for many weeks. My mother, in her desperate attempt to save me, traded those precious bags of rice for antibiotics. I think she thought I might die due to the severity of my condition. To save me she would have traded in everything she had.

I had never really considered surviving the scorpion sting as some "big" miracle from God. But mother told me that she had almost lost all hope. The more I think about it the more convinced I am that my merciful heavenly Father was once again looking out for me.

One day while I was lying on my bed, still suffering from that ferocious fever, I was startled by a bloodcurdling scream. Almost immediately mother and Sopheak came bursting into the room yanking my feeble body off the bed. Mother shouted, "Let's go, the Khmer Rouge is here, and they've just killed some of the children! We've got to get out of here!"

At that point, I had enough sense to know that we were in grave danger, but I was so weak that I could not run. Sopheak was too small to run, so mother had to carry him on her hip. Desperately, she propped me into the back of one of my aunt's ox wagons. Although I was frail, I was fully aware of the chaos that was swirling around me.

People were running everywhere, screaming for their lives and loved ones. As the ox gradually pulled us away from the ghastly scene, we began to approach some bushes. Something caught my attention. I could hear the screams of a baby that was probably abandoned by a distraught mother. The crying seemed to get louder and louder the closer we came. I was shocked as I watched our cart pass by the place from where the cries came. No one stopped or even seemed to hear the helpless infant. Horror-struck by this gruesome reality, I screamed for my mother, who, now, was nowhere in sight. The noise of gunshots and bursting grenades still filled the air. Again, I began to panic, afraid being left alone.

As we continued to roll along the gunfire eventually ceased. Now all I could hear was my own voice screaming for mother. "Mak, where are you? I need you! Where are you, Mak?" Terrible thoughts of having to go through life alone without mother nearly overwhelmed me. But again God spared me from my fears. Somehow, through all the noise and confusion mother found me. Once again, I was safe in her arms.

As I think about my own life I am truly amazed and astonished at the depth, the width, and the height of God's unfailing love for me and my family. His grace is deeper than the deepest sea. His mercy is endless as the East is from the West. His compassion baffles my mind. When I was still a sinner, and did not know of His existence, He reached down time after time and lifted me up from danger and death. What a God! What a Savior! I love my God, because He first loved me!

I love the Lord, for he heard my voice; he heard my cry for mercy. Because he turned his ear to me, I will call on him as long as I live. The cords of death entangled me, the anguish of the grave came upon me; I was overcome by trouble and sorrow. Then I called on the name of the Lord: "O Lord, save me!"
(Psalm 116:1-4)

CHAPTER FOUR

LAUNCHING FOR LIBERTY

*S*hortly after that dreadful battle, mother left us once again with our aunts and uncles. Only this time, she went into Thailand. While the Khmer Rouge was busy battling the Vietnamese soldiers, thousands of Cambodians were using that opportunity to escape to Thailand. Mother and father's youngest brother were among the tens of thousands who sought refuge in our neighboring country. Not long after they arrived at one of the refugee camps along the Thai border mother sent my uncle back for my brother and me. She stayed in Thailand, assisting the Red Cross with landmine victims. This gave her a place to stay and helped her earn food.

Because their special relationship, our uncle willingly risked his own life to return to our devastated homeland to bring us to her. I will be forever grateful to him for his love and sacrifice that ultimately saved our lives. I do not doubt for one moment that it was God who moved upon my uncle's heart to carry out His plan to rescue us from the horrors of the Killing Fields. Although my uncle was not aware of it then, he played a huge part in God's plan for our lives. Who could have imagined, then, what God was orchestrating behind the scenes of our lives.

I can still remember that day when our uncle entered our village with his dilapidated bicycle looking for Sopheak and me. I was beside myself when I heard him say that mother had sent him back to bring us to her. I had wondered if we would ever see our precious mother again. How many innumerable times had I wondered if she had been captured and raped, or even killed by the Khmer Rouge. How delightful it was to hear that not only was she still alive, but that she loved us enough to send for us. I would no longer worry that she had left us behind as orphans forever.

The next evening, our uncle had Sopheak and I say our farewells to our relatives who had been so kind to keep us on behalf of mother. We hopped on his old bicycle and rode off toward the mountain bordering Thailand. Sopheak sat in the basket, off of the handle bar. I sat on the seat holding on tightly to my uncle's waist as he peddled furiously on the jagged roads. The trip to the mountain took hours and finally came to a point where we couldn't ride the bicycle any more. We got off the bicycle to lighten the load so our uncle could push it up the rugged foothills.

During that time, there were millions of land mines planted by the Khmer Rouge along the border and the foothills of the mountains. Therefore, there was no room to be careless. Our uncle had to be very cautious. Every step we took was potentially dangerous. Literally thousands lost either their lives or their limbs to those killer mines. Again, by the grace of God, we were spared any injury.

I am reminded of the many great promises of God recorded in the Book of Psalms. What is even more profound is that He was faithful to me before I knew that He existed. Promises for safety and protection were extended to me then while I was still an ignorant child. Talk about the incomprehensible and unconditional love of such a merciful God!

> *"Surely he will save you from the fowler's snare and from the deadly pestilence. He will cover you with his feathers, and under his wings you will find refuge; his faithfulness will be your shield and rampart. You will not fear the terror of night, nor the arrow that flies by day, nor the pestilence that stalks in the darkness, nor the plaque that destroys at midday. A thousand my fall at your side, ten thousand at your right hand, but it will not come near you"*
> (Psalm 91:3-7).

The trip crossing over the mountain into Thailand was brutal. Especially for my uncle, since he was responsible for all three of us. I don't recall being scared except at night when it got dark. There was not much talking, only our uncle whispering to us to be silent as we crawled through particular areas where there were signs of a possible Khmer Rouge campsite. Then we would dash from bush to bush dodging the bright moonlight from revealing our position to our enemies.

The most frightening moments were times when we had to be completely still and almost breathless as uncle put his big hands over our mouths. All I would hear was my own heart beating rapidly as my mind was filled with fears of the Khmer Rouge catching us and slicing out throats like they did to those children in our village back home. But fortunately, we were not discovered by our enemies. It was definitely God hiding us underneath His wings of protection. When we got desperate in need of rest, we slept on the ground surrounded by thickets as our shelter to regain strength for the remaining journey ahead.

After resting for what seemed like such a short time, we left our hiding place and started again for the border. I remember running beside uncle as he pushed the bicycle as quietly as possible through the dark night. All of a sudden, we came upon to some water. I can still see the shinny ripples as the moonlight glistened on the surface. My earlier experiences with leeches and dead bodies, however, left me afraid of the water. The fact that I couldn't swim hardly crossed my mind.

I have no way of telling how wide or deep that water was, but somehow or another, Uncle Saang managed to swim to the other side with me and Sopheak clinging to his back. I guess you could say we became like leeches on his back. Now that I think about it I don't remember how he got his bicycle across. I guess he must have had to make two trips that night, one for us and one for the bicycle. Regardless, uncle got us safely to the shore.

*"He reached down from on high and took hold of me;
he drew me out of deep waters. He rescued me from my
powerful enemy, from my foes, who were too strong for me.*

They confronted me in the day of my disaster, but
the Lord was my support. He brought me into a spacious place;
he rescued me because he delighted in me"
(Psalm 18:16-19).

We hurried along all night with little rest. We kept up that pace until rays from the radiant sun pierced through the forest cover. We were descending from the mountains and would soon be entering our neighboring nation of Thailand. I remember being on my bicycle perch with uncle swiftly peddling us through the jungle. Our frantic dash toward mother and freedom thrilled my soul. But once again, my excitement was interrupted when I detected another unpleasant smell. Quickly, my thoughts raced back into my recent past. "I've smelled this stench before! Could it be another dead body?" I pondered silently as I clung tightly to my uncle.

Within moments the grotesque odor became undeniably real. There, beside the path, lay the corpse of some lost soul whose final dream was freedom on the other side of the border. Unfortunately, he never lived to realize his aspiration. Like the many other war-weary souls attempting to escape the Killing Fields, he too had perished.

I could tell that my uncle had no intention of stopping anywhere near that corpse. But my curiosity overcame my good sense and I begged our uncle to stop for a moment. I pestered him until he slowed down enough for me to take a look. Why would I want to approach casualty? I'm not certain but it was probably because I wanted so desperately to find my missing father. I needed to find him and I needed to know, once and for all was he dead or alive!

But father wasn't lying there that day rotting in the hot sun. Judging by his condition, the lifeless soul must have been killed just days prior. Thank God we were not with him in that death zone when the end came! Again, our steps definitely seemed ordered by the Lord. Our timing couldn't have been better because it was actually God's timing—to bring us safely through, after, and not during the attack.

Finally, we reached the refugee camp. Uncle Saang delivered us safely and happily into our mother's waiting arms. Were we ever thrilled to be with her again! I thought, "At last, we are together to live happily ever after!" With mother back in our lives the world immediately became brighter. We were now safe in a war-free land. We couldn't ask for anything more—except having daddy with us as well. He was the missing part that would have made our family complete. Then it would have been heaven on earth for me!

We lived in a little hut sown together by branches and vines and covered with straw. The bed we had to sleep on was made out of wooden boards. While it was not the most comfortable bed I've slept on I was especially thankful that I no longer had to sleep on the ground with jungle critters. To my young mind, I thought we were finally out of danger and ready to move up in the world.

Every morning, mother would give us some money to go to the market and purchase food. We could buy what ever we wanted. I would always order my favorite noodle dish with a delicious sweet and sour sauce. One day Mother took Sopheak and me to the market and bought me a little doll on a string. My little doll had a pretty yellow dress. She was cheerful as well as beautiful! I suppose that is when yellow became my favorite color. Once more we were happy and laughing together. Life was relatively good considering all that we had been through!

During the days, mother would spend most of her time inside the blue hospital tent working as a nurse's assistant. Sometimes, I would join her and observe her as she assisted landmine victims. I watched her sew up a man's leg that had been blown off. He was bleeding uncontrollably and was in excruciating pain lying there helplessly on the operating table. I saw the white jagged bone protruding from out of his torn flesh. Curious children were pushing aggressively against the tent trying to see all that was going on. I felt extra special because I was inside the tent with mother with a direct view of all the action.

At some point, the nosey brats got so loud that it agitated me. In my anger I picked up one of the large needles that mother used to stitch up wounds, and began stabbing the sides of the tent. I heard the children yelling out in pain as the needle jabbed into their hands. Little by little the noise settled down as each injured child ran off crying for their mothers to comfort them. All of those working that day must have been too busy to notice my destructive outburst.

Looking back, I wished someone would have noticed and given me a good spanking for what I had done.

I remember one particular young soldier who was assisting mother in the tent that day. He helped perform the amputation on that land mine victim. He wasn't a doctor. I noticed him because he seemed to hang around us quite a bit. Mother had introduced Sopheak and me to him when we first got there, but I thought nothing of him at first.

It wasn't long, however, before I had begun to put two and two together. I concluded that he was up to no good. He was always trying to speak to our young, beautiful mother and I did not like that one bit, regardless of how nice he was trying to be to us.

He tried to soften our hearts toward him by bringing us food, candies, soda and toys. He even gave us money to go to the market. He repeatedly tried to make small talk with us and bribe us with gifts. But I knew in my heart, that he was just like all those other men. All he wanted was our beautiful mother. I knew exactly what he was up to because I had seen it so many times before. I knew I needed to come up with a plan to get rid of him once and for all.

In my strong dislike for him, I came up with my battle plan. I enlisted my little brother, Sopheak as my combat-partner to help me execute my mission. I concluded that it was time to make our position known. No more sweet bribes for us! It was time to declare war on our detestable enemy. He had enjoyed his last flirtations with our mother. I had developed such a dislike for him that I could hardly handle his presence anywhere near our mother or near us.

Finally the day had arrived for us to put our plan into action. We caught him one day speaking to mother right in front of our house. Irate, I went to a nearby palm tree and tore off two sturdy branches. I gave one to Sopheak and kept the other for myself. With weapons in hands, we bolted toward our enemy who was unashamedly serenading our mother with his sweet talk. Like a fearless lion, I was ready to devour my prey. With a loud, forceful war cry, I shouted out a command and Sopheak and I launched our frontal attacked.

Sopheak took one side, and I took the other. Without mercy, we beat our enemy with our palm branches. Ferociously, I struck and kicked him everywhere I could. While we were beating him madly

I screamed, "Don't you ever speak to my mother again! I will kill you! I hate you!"

Mother was stunned! She could not believe that her two little precious children could deliver such a barrage of hatred and violence upon her unsuspecting suitor. She pleaded for us to stop beating up on him. We didn't stop immediately, but eventually out of respect for mother, we released our enemy. After our retreat, embarrassed nearly to tears, mother profusely apologized to her friend for having to endure such punishment. Little did we know that the soldier we ambushed that day would one day become our step-father.

After that ambush, mother demanded a truce and Sopheak and I were all forced to be at peace with our enemy. For a short but peaceful time we resided there with mother at the Red Cross camp. Then one sunny day, without any warning, someone threw a grenade into the midst of our safe haven. It exploded right outside of our little hut. Mother was not around, and my brother and I began to cry. Horror-struck, Sopheak and I crawled underneath our bed and held tightly to each other as we whimpered in each other's arms.

Yet again, our peaceful refuge had turned into a chaotic blood-bath with people everywhere running and screaming for their lives and looking for their loved ones. All I could think about was the horrific sound of the gunfire and thundering explosions that were bursting right outside our hut. Would we fall victim to the next bomb or grenade? But much to my relief, mother came rushing in, yelling out our names and frantically searching for us. Hearing her voice, at that riotous moment, brought much needed comfort to our hearts. Quickly we crawled out from underneath the bed as she wrapped her arms around our trembling bodies.

Without a moment to waste, we ran out of our little haven, joining other terrified souls running once again for our very lives. This time, the bullets and grenades were aimed at a different enemy. The North Vietnamese soldiers and the Khmer Rouge were in the midst of a heated battle. It was impossible to know which way to run or who was trying to kill whom. We had no idea which way to run. But we knew that if we didn't run like everyone else, we would definitely be dead.

Like the many others, we darted for the shelter that would most likely shield us from this present danger. I cannot remember exactly which direction we ran or how long that battle lasted. I don't know who won the battle. But once the fighting ceased and everything had quieted down, mother once again arranged to send us away to a safer place.

When I think back upon the bloodshed from the attack of that day, once again I find myself utterly amazed at the love and mercy God had for us then. What undeserving grace that He extended to mother, Sopheak and me. I am taken aback to think how very close that grenade dropped—jut a few feet from us. Yet, there we were, untouched! I am astounded that God would choose to shield us. I cannot possibly express with words my thankfulness to Him for the mercies He persistently poured upon me. I can only testify that God, my Creator is unquestionably a merciful Father. Just as His words promise His loving kindness for His beloved creations truly endures forever.

"The Lord is gracious and righteous; our God is full of compassion. The Lord protects the simple hearted; when I was in great need, he saved me"
(Psalm 116:5-6).

CHAPTER FIVE

JESUS IN THE REFUGEE CAMP

Following the attack, mother took Sopheak and me to Kau-I-Dang refugee camp to live with our daddy's mother. In Kau-I-Dang, living conditions were a bit more secure. Mother explained to grandma that the camp where we had been was too dangerous. She asked grandma if she could entrust us with them while she was gone for a short period of time. She assured us that she would return to get us. Because of a previous promise and to honor her son's last wish, grandmother agreed to take both of us in temporarily. Once they came to terms, mother soon left us with grandma. Once more, our hearts would ache intensely from missing her and wanting her with us.

It was early 1979 when Sopheak and I joined our new family in Kau-I-Dang. It was at that time that grandma began taking Sopheak and me to meet with some of the village palm readers. She wanted to inquire about daddy's fate. She would sacrifice whatever little change she could find to pay the psychics to tell us if father was dead or alive. She seemed driven to know if her son was still alive somewhere or had already been killed. It was an emotional tug-of-war for all of us, as one psychic would tell us that daddy was alive, and the next would tell us that he had been killed. One day we might walk away filled with hope and the next filled with grief.

As time went on, the pain of missing my parents seemed to subside. Sometimes, it seemed I could go for days or even weeks without thinking about them. I found myself happy, playing, and laughing once again with our new family and friends in our new surroundings. Our new family was comprised of six: our step-grandfather, our grandma, an older cousin, our youngest aunt, Sopheak and me.

Like my brother and me, our cousin was also an orphan. She had been tragically separated from her family during the war. To save herself, she escaped Cambodia with other family members and came to Thailand. Our aunt was grandma and grandpa's youngest daughter. She was only three years older than me. At the time, I was nearly eight years old, and Sopheak was almost seven years old. Grandma and grandpa were in their late fifties and had their hands full.

Life wasn't too bad without our parents. I became quite a cheerful little camper as time passed. I was drawing closer to my step-grandfather. He was quite a man. All the children knew him as the camp's storyteller. All the village children loved his stories and jokes and would surround him, listening contently and laughing at all of his silly jokes.

Sometimes he would try to bribe the children to get them to bum a cigarette off their parents. I guess it was his way of being compensated for making them laugh. I was especially captivated by grandpa's young, entertaining, and cheerful personality. I found him so funny that I would roll around on the ground with laughter until my belly ached. He taught me how to do body massages by practicing on him. I was like a little sponge soaking up his many stories and experiences. I found myself hanging on to his every word. He intrigued me to the point that I even stopped missing my own father. I guess I was having too much fun to be sad over daddy. Unknowingly, grandpa had begun to take the place of my missing father. He became my new hero, the apple of my eye. I adored him with all my heart.

One day, grandpa received an opportunity to earn some extra wages to support our family of six. He took a job as a water-jar potter outside of the camps. The position required him to stay at the worksite during the week, but he was able to come home on weekends to be with the family. By that time I had gotten so attached to him that I couldn't bear being without him all week long. I did not want to be without my best friend. He was my world! So, I begged grandma to let me go to his worksite with him. Grandpa told grandma that it was alright; that he wanted me to go with him. So she finally agreed to my requests. Ecstatically, I jumped on grandpa's back and off toward his new job we went. How special I felt to have grandpa all to myself. I just adored him.

When we arrived at grandpa's jobsite we put our claim on where we would be sleeping. Our bed was little more than a few boards with mosquito netting draped over them. I don't remember very much about that place or how long we stayed there but I do remember being right by his side helping him while he worked, and chatting with him as though I was one of the other men in the group. We worked together everyday and I eagerly anticipated the day's end when grandpa and I could play together. The highlights of my days were playing with him after work. It was so much fun to be with him!

Every evening after work, once we were finished with our supper, we would get in our bed, pull down the net and start playing our games. He'd begin telling me his funny stories and I would laugh, and laugh, and laugh like there wasn't a care in the world. He seemed to be able to drown all of my sorrow with joy and laughter. I remember him tickling me so hard that I would burst out kicking and laughing hysterically. I'd laugh so hard, it would hurt. Then I would beg him to stop, so he would stop for a moment to let me catch my breath. After a moments rest I would jump gleefully all over him again. The other men sharing our room just stared at us and wondered what we were doing. We had such fun together!

Many times, after a long, hard day at work, grandpa would ask me to massage his back. Then he would offer to massage me. I loved getting massages from grandpa. He was my master teacher who taught me how to give good massages. He always commended me on my good work. He told me all the time how smart I was and that I was his favorite grandchild! His compliments and affirmation were everything that my sad and lonely heart needed to hear. His approval gave me inspiration and strength to cope with my missing parents.

His love filled an empty place in my life! But I am embarrassed to admit that during many of our playtimes together; the tickling became less than appropriate.

Too many times, grandpa's tickles and massages became intimate touches. In my childhood innocence I did not fully understand that what grandpa was doing was wrong. I accepted it as part of playing together. So, I had no reason to run away from him or ask him to stop. He was my best friend. He was the friend who turned my gloomy world upside down and filled it with laughs. He was everything to me!

In 1980, missionaries came to the Kau-I-Dang refugee camps to try to bring relief to traumatized refugees like our family. Grandma, being a Buddhist worshipper, was not impressed with their teachings that Jesus Christ was the Lord and Savior of the Cambodian people. Like the millions of other Cambodians, grandma believed that each nation had their own native god. She also believed that each nation should only worship the god of their ancestors according to their own customs and traditions. Worshipping foreign gods was a high crime. It was treason!

I'd often overheard her comments about our countrymen who had converted to Christianity because of the work of the missionaries in our camps. She, along with other Buddhists, was quick to accuse the new Cambodian Christians of being traitors to their country and to Buddha. Grandma determined that Cambodian Christians had lost their sanity. She found it repulsive that they would deny Buddha, the god of their ancestors, to exalt Jesus Christ, a foreign God. Living in a foreign land did not justify them in abandoning their religion. In her heart, she swore that she would never betray Buddha like those other traitors.

Well, it appeared as though this foreign God, Jesus Christ, was out to prove grandma wrong. There was a time when grandma's youngest daughter, became seriously ill. She had severe fevers and was terribly sick. For many days and nights grandma's precious daughter had showed no signs of improvement. Grandma, bound by her traditions, naturally sought out the village doctor to come recite their healing rituals over her sick child. The witch doctor called out to their ancestors, and mixed up a concoction of roots and herbal medicine for her to drink. Grandma invited the monks to chant their prayers and she also prayed day and night to Buddha to heal her daughter. But all her efforts, as well as the efforts of the witch doctors and monks, proved futile. She saw no signs of relief or improvement in her beloved daughter's health.

Out of her desperation, she finally called out to the foreign God that the missionaries were proclaiming. She struck a deal with him by saying, "Lord Jesus, if you really are the one and true God, please heal my daughter! If you heal her, then I will believe that you are my God!" With this vow, she went into the village church and requested for the elders of the church to come pray for her daughter. Delighted, the elders responded to her appeal and followed her back to our hut.

Upon arrival, the elders anointed my aunt with oil. I also saw them sprinkle her body with a light blessing shower and offer up prayers on her behalf. They walked back and forth in our little hut praying and interceding on her behalf to the Lord. Once they had finished praying, the elders encouraged grandma to come to church once her daughter was healed. When they left my aunt was still lying there comatose. But grandma noticed that almost at once her daughter's feverish body was cooling down. Exhausted from the stress and lack of sleep from our prolonged ordeal, we all lie down and fell asleep.

During the night we were awakened by a startling cry, "Mak, there was a man standing by my bed! There was a man, and he touched me!" We were all shock to see my aunt speaking again. She appeared to be well. Needless to say, we were exuberant over this miracle. Grandma began praising her new God, Jesus Christ, and proclaimed Him as the one and true God who had answered her desperate cry. The next morning, she took all of us to the church and dedicated each of us to our newfound God. There is no question that my aunt's healing was a pivotal point in our family's Christian heritage. Thank you grandma and thank you Jesus!

Because of God's miraculous intervention in our family, we became heavily involved with other Christians at the church. We came to church faithfully to study the Bible and learning about our new God. Now it was our family who suddenly become the brunt of mocking and jokes for our surrounding neighbors. Now we were the ones who were committing treason against Buddha. I'm sure it wasn't easy for grandma to bare their remarks and ridicule at times but for her there was no turning back. She had seen the mighty power of God and wasn't about to go back to a god who couldn't save her daughter.

Grandma brought us to Sunday school where we would sing in the children's choir and do our special presentations for the holidays. Learning about God's grace and salvation gave us hope for a better life. It felt like we had not only a new life but a new freedom as well. It was like we were no longer living under life's heavy burdens and oppression; things that at one time had us imprisoned like flies caught in a spider's web.

For the first time, I began to sense that there was a ray of light in the midst of the deadly darkness that we had been in for so long. I felt joy in my heart and was aware of the drastic change in all of our countenances, especially grandma. She was so caught up with learning God's Word she enlisted me as her study partner. Together, grandma and I studied God's word passionately. Together we read the Scriptures and practiced writing it in our Cambodian language.

As the message of the Gospel began to sink into my heart, I began to believe that there was actually "goodness" in the world and not merely evil. I first saw goodness, gentleness, compassion and tenderness expressed through the loving missionaries. The Jesus in them made my sad heart smile once again. Sopheak and I, along with dozens of other war-torn children, swarmed to them like bees on a honeycomb. They took time to minister to us, freely sharing the love and attention of which we had been so deprived.

I remember one very special missionary who taught me songs about the goodness of Jesus. She was like a beautiful angel sent just to love on me personally. I became so deeply and emotionally attached to her that my heart cried out, "Please be my mother! Please love me as your own child!" I reached the place where I never ever wanted to be without her. Now, I realize that the cry of my heart for the woman of God was really a cry for the God that she was serving. The God that my wonderful missionary friend was serving was irresistible. It was His love that flowed through her to me. And it was His love that lifted my desolate soul so that I did not want to live without it. He was calling out to me through her to experience His great love. But at that point in my life I didn't recognize my Shepherd's voice. My eyes were fixed on His servant and not on the Master, Himself.

The tender love and sacrifices that the missionaries made provoked my curious mind to ask questions like, "What are they here for? We have nothing to offer them! We are refugees! What could these wonderfully kind people possibly gain from doing all these good deeds for destitute refugees?" Then, somehow, these questions caused my impressionable mind to ignite new thoughts about the existence and reality of the God they served—this Jesus Christ, His Son.

They told us that Jesus Christ is the Savior of the world who died for us in order to save us from hell. The many films the missionaries show us explained his birth, life and eventual death upon the cross. "Well, if these people are good, it is because their God is good!" So while in the depth of my despair, I began to realize a hope for a better future if only I would put my hope in the man on the cross! How grateful I am, to this day, for those loving missionaries that God sent to relieve my pain, and the pain of my people. I was impacted for eternity because I found hope in the Jesus in them at a time when it was impossible to hope at all.

It seemed like months had passed since mother left us. It might have even been a whole year since we saw her last. One day, during school, an attractive young woman came into our classroom and interrupted our class. As she spoke quietly to our teacher the students wondered in awe about the stranger. All the while, I was also busy gazing at all the lovely features of the intriguing lady. I especially took noticed of her pretty face and delicate hands, as well as her long thick black hair that hung down to her waist. Her beauty captivated me.

As I casually observed the lovely stranger whispering into my teacher's ear, a shadowy memory passed through my mind. Then I realized it was the ring the lovely stranger was wearing. I thought to myself, that ring sure looks familiar. I wonder if she could be my mother. As I pondered that possibility, I felt my heart thumping with excitement. Then all of a sudden, to my greatest delight, my teacher called, "Sopheak and Lakhina, come and greet your mother!"

Exploding with sheer ecstasy, we both bolted like lightning to embrace our long-missed mother. We wrapped our arms around her waist and legs greeting her with tears of pure joy. The teacher dismissed us from class that day to spend some much needed and precious reunion time with our beloved mother.

We were beside our selves that day, hopping and skipping along beside mother. All the way home we kept telling her how much we loved her and had missed her. Proudly, I shouted to neighbors as we were passing by, "Hey, this is my mother! Isn't she beautiful? She is my mother!" I wanted all the people to know that I was not an orphan like they believed. I was beyond delighted to prove those ugly rumors wrong—that mother would never return to us.

There was no doubt in my mind that this reunion with mother would be final; once and for all. Having her homecoming meant happy days had finally returned for our little family! At last, I had my own family! I didn't need to borrow our grandmother or the missionary to be my mother anymore. Neither my family nor the neighbors could call Sopheak and me orphans.

All that week, I made sure everyone in the community, young and old, met my beautiful mother. I was especially proud of the fact that mother's return proved of her love for us. I was relieved to see that mother did not abandon us like many predicted. I felt safe and satisfied having her presence in my world once again bringing comfort to my delicate heart.

Sopheak and I did not know it but it wasn't in mother's plan to stay with us permanently on that particular trip. Like the many before it was just a temporary visit. Now she was only making one of her periodic guest appearances into our lives. Later we learned that on her next visit she was planning to take both Sopheak and me with her permanently. She told grandma and my aunt that she had important business to take care of first but then she would surely return for us once and for all. My young mind did not understand how she could torment our fragile hearts with empty promises. I simply could not comprehend how "other business" was more important than Sopheak and me.

Looking back at that precarious time, I must have had some sort of premonition of that dreadful day when she would leave us again. Maybe her pattern had simply become so embedded in my heart and thoughts that I just learned to expect the inevitable. I really don't know how I knew, but I sensed toward the end of the week that she might pull another disappearing trick on us again.

A few days later, while we were all standing outside, that frightful thought of losing mother came over me. The way mother and grandma were talking and occasionally casting a look my way, I felt like they were up to something; something they did not want us children to know. In my confusion and fear I grabbed mother and cried out, "Mak, please don't leave us! Please don't leave us again, Mak!" At the same time Sopheak join in on the other side pulling and pleading for her not to leave us. Moved by our desperate whimpering, grandma began to cry tears of compassion and also plead with mother not to leave us.

Mother seemed unmoved by our tearful requests. She told Sopheak and me that it would be okay. Then she told us to turn around to watch the birds flying in the sky. She said, "Look over there! Look at those birds soaring in the sky!" I felt that it was a trick and resisted at first because I was afraid that if I took my eyes off of her she would disappear. Still, in spite of my fear and out of a trusting heart, I turned around with Sopheak to look at the birds flying in the sky.

I didn't see any birds flying anywhere near us at all. I just remember that once we turned back around, mother was gone! Once more, we found ourselves wailing with heart-wrenching pain from the agony of her betrayal.

Months later, after we had transferred to a different camp with grandma and the rest of our family, we learned that mother tried to come back to Kau-I-Dang for us. But she was too late! Thailand had closed its borders to Cambodian refugees. No one could have known that mother's fateful decision to leave us would separate us for a very long time. The effects of that one choice would ultimately extend over continents, oceans and time. It would be nearly three decades before Sopheak and I would see our beloved mother again.

CHAPTER SIX

FAREWELL MY HERO AND HOMELAND!

In late 1980 we moved once again. This time our new home was at the Kamput refugee camp in Thailand. At Kamput we were reunited with Uncle Saang, the one who brought us through that dangerous journey from Cambodia. Only this time, my uncle was no longer single and the eight of us had to live together in a tiny house. I was thrilled to be able to go back to school once again. When we were not in school, grandma would send Sopheak and me to the market place to sell candies, homemade snacks, desserts and vegetables. She did this to bring extra money to buy meat, fish or rice. I became a traveling salesgirl complete with a basket of goodies on my head. My little brother was my business partner. His job was to locate customers. Crossing from one sandy road to the next, we would call out to passerby like circus concessionaires selling their goods. Rarely did we return until everything was sold. Grandma was so proud of us when we returned with an empty basket having been so successful. We would give her the profits from the day and she never failed to pay us generously—with compliments, "You're so smart and so useful!" Her encouragement delighted my heart and motivated me to try to do even more for her.

One day, quite by surprise, we received a letter. Since I was the eager reader of the family, grandma gave it to me to read out loud to the rest of the family. The letter was from one of father's childhood friends and a close friend of our family. Although I didn't know him, grandma and uncle knew him well. The man served with daddy in the Cambodian military. It was thrilling just to hear grandma tell us that the man knew my daddy. My heart began to bubble with excitement and anticipation. I longed for any information there was about my missing father. So, I began to eagerly read to reach the part where he would tell us where daddy was.

I guess one reason I was so excited was because during our stay in the refugee camps I had personally witnessed numbers of families reunited with lost loved ones. This had caused my hope for finding daddy to rise. My expectations were high because I believed, with all of my heart, that daddy would soon be reunited with us. I was sure that this letter would reveal to me where daddy was and that he had been searching for us. Surely, we were going to find daddy at last.

Optimistically I read through the greeting and first paragraph. Daddy's friend reported that he and daddy, along with some other soldier friends, had escaped from the Khmer Rogue. Realizing that the Khmer Rouge was getting ready to execute them, they made a collective decision to stand together and fight for their lives. They knew quite well that they had nothing to lose but much to gain.

"Wow! This is remarkable news!" My heart leapt with joy as I proceeded to read. My excitement was short-lived, however, when the news took a definite turn for the worse. In fact, the direction it took was horrific; causing me to face a grim reality for which my confident heart could have never been prepared.

He said that they were initially successful in their resistance against the Khmer Rouge and had escaped from their captors. They were able to break away but the story did not end there.

The conclusion of their heroic effort did not, regrettably, conclude with a happily-ever-after ending. After their escape they made their way in the direction of Thailand in hopes of finding freedom. Weakened and still bound with ropes the men plodded wearily toward safety on the other side of the border. My daddy's friend wrote that, one by one, his companions collapsed and died. Imprisonment under the Khmer Rouge was harsh. Life in the concentration camps was brutal and their treacherous journey into Thailand was simply devastating. He shared his deepest regrets of how truly sorry he was that his close childhood friend, my daddy, was one of the many that had perished along the mountainsides. He said that out of the group my father was in he was the only one who made it to Thailand alive.

Suddenly, my soul seemed to erupt in one intense and torturous flame. Heart broken, I let out a scream for my dead father. Suddenly, my world came crashing down. It seemed like every fiber of my being had been torn and all I wanted to do was to go find my father's corpse, lie down next to him, and die.

I could see no reason to go on living. All the dreams I had of being reunited with my father and hero were gone. Fear of the unknown began ravaging my mind. How would I live without him? How would I survive? Who would be there to take care of me and protect me from the lightning storms of life? My daddy had been my ultimate comfort, my security, and my protector! What would happen to me now?

I have never known pain so deep and so excruciating as what I experienced that day. I wailed aloud with pure anguish, "Pa! My pa is dead! Pa, you have left me! You've died and abandoned me, Pa!" I screamed, grief stricken, until I couldn't scream anymore.

Numbness engulfed me as I lay motionless in the pool of my own tears. I could not bring myself to accept the chilling fact that daddy was no longer alive. I couldn't stop seeing, in my mind, pictures of my beloved father lying dead along a trail like so many other poor souls I had seen. Daddy was a good person! How could something as horrible and evil happen to someone as wonderful as he? I know my pitiful cries must have pierced the heart of God that day!

All I wanted was to be able to go to him. If I could just see him and wrap my arms around him and tell him how much I loved him! If I could be there, maybe it wouldn't be so bad! He wouldn't have to be alone! How could my precious father die in such a wicked way?

He was gone, leaving only the echoes of his contagious laughter reverberating somewhere in the recesses of my mind. As time passed, I began to dwell on the harsh reality of never being able to see daddy's smiling face smile again and I would become overwhelmed. I would begin to scream and wail all over again until there were no more tears and no more strength in me to make a sound.

It broke grandma's heart as well as she grieved over her lost son. She would wrap her tender arms around my trembling body and gently stroked my hair, wiping away my tears along with her own. I could see that my grandmother shared and understood the depth of my pain. Her loss was as great as mine. But she was just stronger than me and better at dealing with her sorrow.

I can't explain how deep the wounds of daddy's death left on our hearts. Talking about daddy's death was not something that my brother and I ever did. I can't remember my brother ever opening up and sharing his feelings about our father's death. He says he does not remember him at all. I guess in a way, it is probably best. I know he misses not having a daddy when he was growing up. But I am glad that he will never have to feel the bitter sting of death from losing daddy like I did.

I did not know the Healer of the brokenhearted in those days, and consequently my suffering was brutal. I bore the wretched pain of losing daddy without relief. I was not aware that there was, in fact, a God that could help relieve my pain and suffering; a God who could heal my hemorrhaging heart. I did not know that He could take such a shattered heart and piece it back together and make it whole.

Furthermore, I had no idea that He even wanted to heal me and save me from my torment. I was unable then to understand that Father God could actually take my daddy's place in my life and become the Father that I so desperately needed. I did not know that the all-powerful God who lives in heaven wanted to be my Daddy until two decades after my father's death! Once I began to understand God's heart toward me, I began to comprehend His willingness to become a Father to the fatherless. This powerful revelation ultimately helped me deal with daddy's death as well as the many other brutal storms of life I've faced since then.

While I did not know about God and His love, He certainly knew all about me and all about my needs. I am convinced that because of His infinite mercy and love, God reached out to me and helped me in my darkest hours. His unfailing love was present during those catastrophic moments in my life. He loved me by giving me grace to walk through all those horrible experiences, even through the valley of the shadow of death itself. Countless times He proved His love for me by snatching me out of the grasp of death.

The unbelievable fact about my awesome God is that He was there for me when I didn't even know that He existed. Had I known how much He loved a pitiful little orphan like me, surely I would have asked Him to comfort my aching heart. The miracle is this: He helped me when I did not know that He was my heavenly Father and He loved me so much that He longed to be my Hero, my Protector, and my Provider. I didn't know then that He could meet my physical, emotional and spiritual needs. It wasn't until much later in my life that I discovered that I could run to Him for salvation and protection, and because of my lack of knowledge, I chose to live in my bitterness instead of embracing God's restoration.

> *"Though my father and mother forsake me,*
> *the Lord will receive me"*
> (Psalm 27:10).

> *"I will be a Father to you, and you will be my*
> *sons and daughters, says the Lord Almighty"*
> (2 Corinthians 6:18).

Looking back from where I am now, I believe my daddy's death dealt a crippling blow to my fragile heart in that season of my young life. The harsh reality of losing the most significant person in my life forced me to put away my childhood innocence and tenderness. It was as though I became another person. Somehow, a new child was birthed in me and from that moment forward, the new me was ruled by a different spirit. This spirit was a warring spirit that wanted blood in exchange for all the suffering, hurt and pain that life had dealt me. Anybody who would try to hurt my brother or me would pay dearly.

In my anger, I unleashed a hellish wrath on people who knowingly or unknowingly disturbed those festering emotional wounds I suffered in those early, brutal years of my life. I was blinded by my hatred and an enormous thirst for vengeance. Yet, in my mind I was blameless. I was so obsessed by all the evil committed by the Khmer Rouge, that I was able to conveniently overlook the evil in my own soul. I could not see that the very things that I despised in them were the same things that filled my own deceitful heart. Attempting to justify my evil attitudes and actions I was actually as guilty as Pol Pot and the Khmer Rouge. I was as eager to "shed blood" as they had ever been.

"As it is written: 'There is no one righteous, not even one; there is no one who understands, no one who seeks God. All have turned away, they have together become worthless; there is no one who does good, not even one. Their throats are open graves; their tongues practice deceit. The poison of vipers is on their lips. Their mouths are full of cursing and bitterness." "Their feet are swift to shed blood; ruin and misery mark their ways, and the way of peace they do not know." "There is no fear of God before their eyes'"
(Roman 3:10).

I wish I knew then what I know now—someone had already made full reparation for my sin, suffering, and pain. His name was Jesus, the Son of God! The Bible calls him, "the Lamb of God, slain before the foundation of the world." In order to satisfy God's righteous demands on mankind it meant there had to be a sinless sacrifice. "…without the shedding of blood there is no forgiveness of sins" (Hebrews 9:22). So, God appointed His sinless Son, Jesus Christ, to die on the cross for the sins of the world. That means Jesus paid debt mankind could never pay and ultimately died for the very ones I despised; the very ones who took my daddy away from me.

"For God did not appoint us to suffer wrath but to receive salvation through our Lord Jesus Christ. He died for us that, whether we are awake or asleep, we may live together with him"
(1 Thessalonians 5:9-10).

Because I did not understand these things, I harbored all that hate and unforgiveness needlessly. I was determined to make sure that others paid dearly for what I had suffered. Ultimately, anger, bitterness, hate and unforgiveness began to consume me and turn my tender heart into stone. Harboring these toxic feelings only opened the door for more curses to come into my life. For the next twenty years, I lived in bondage to the raw emotions that took over my soul. As a result I choose the way marked "death" instead of the way marked "life." Convoluted choices brought me to the place where even the words I spoke were words of death and my actions formed life patterns with horrible consequences.

With my father gone and without mother to help us, Sopheak and I were relegated to the status of orphans. During that first agonizingly week after learning that daddy had died, the pain inside my heart was so intense that I cried throughout the night. Grandma would come to me and take me up into her arms and stroked my hair until I would whimper myself to sleep. Eventually the tears dried up and I was once again able to face reality without my great hero.

Being orphans put us in a different category from other children. In my eyes, I thought that we were just like the rest of the kids in our camps. It wasn't so! Daddy's death put us into a new category, with new kind of names and new labels. I remember grandma referring to my brother and me as "little orphans." In fact she rarely called us by our given names. Now my challenge was to come to the understanding that Sopheak and I were no longer "normal" children. In our culture we had become the "less fortunate" children; "pitiful orphans" who needed sympathy. It wasn't easy but I began to accept my new role and fate as an "unfortunate, pitiful orphan child."

In our Cambodian culture, orphans are considered wild, unruly children who do not know right from wrong. Orphans are viewed as street rats! As a matter of fact, that's the nickname for parentless children like me. Like rats, orphans had to scramble and gather scraps from under the tables and from people's garbage to meet their needs. Orphans were considered to be uncouth, improper and uneducated because they did not have a mature adult to train them. This stigma, over the next decade, resulted in the loss of many valuable relationships with special friends due to the negative influence of their parents. After all, I was a despised orphan. I have tasted the bias and discrimination that exists against the orphans of the world.

In 1981, we were transferred from Kamput to another camp in Chunbori, Thailand. I was about nine years old at the time. In spite of our circumstances as refugees, we had a pretty good life. We were much safer there since Chunbori was out of the war zone. We didn't have to worry about sudden bombardments in the middle of the afternoon or being raided by Khmer Rouge gorillas anymore.

We had the opportunity to attend school and study in safe classroom settings. It was there where I learned how to cook my first pot of rice and experienced my first training as a homemaker. Sopheak and I kept the house for our family while they were out working. Gathering dry twigs from the foothills for the fire to cook our pot of rice was part of our responsibility along with making sure the rice was cooked before the rest of the family got home. I'll never forget the tormenting smoke and how it persistently stung our eyes as we took turns blowing on the tiny embers trying to bring them to life. This memory alone will forever cause me to raise my hands and praise God for my electric rice cooker! Thank you, Jesus!

In Chunbori, our family began the complicated process of applying to immigrate to America. We failed the examination on repeated occasions due to the fact that Sopheak and I were so young. Grandma told us to tell the officials that we were their children, but we always ended up telling them that we did not have any parents. But eventually, by God's grace, we passed the examinations and got our sponsorship to the United States of America.

> *"He has shown his people the power of his works,*
> *giving them the lands of other nations"*
> (Psalm 111:6).

We were on our way to the land of the free but none of us realized that it was God, behind the scenes, orchestrating His plans. It may be difficult to understand but leaving our Asian roots was not a happy occasion; it was quite the contrary. While we were grateful for our opportunity to come to America and hopefully enjoy a better life, leaving our land of birth behind was agonizingly painful. I remember it vividly as I sat there in the airplane moments before taking off to come to America. I felt as though my heart was being ripped out of my chest. I literally wanted to crawl into a cave and die. For me, in that season of my life, coming to America meant death to all of my hopes and dreams of ever being reunited with my beloved mother. It meant farewell to the only world that I had ever known.

My mind was tormented with questions like, "When will I ever see mother again? Will I ever be able to return to my native soil again? Will we ever be able to come back home?" My heart was so heavy that not even grandma could comfort me. I wouldn't be surprised if every person on our plane experienced the same grief as I did as we prepared to leave our birth home for a strange land. After spending a few nights in the Philippines we flew on to Alaska. Finally we entered America on December 17, 1981.

CHAPTER SEVEN

THE LAND OF THE LIVING

It was a cold snowy night in December 1981 when our family arrived in Alaska. I must say that I thank God that Alaska was not our final destination because the temperature was insanely freezing. I saw steam coming out from my nose and mouth for the first time in my life. The cold was almost unbearable to my fragile fifty-pound frame. I was a tropical creature from a tropical country and didn't know what to make of all the ice and snow. How anything, other than polar bears and seals survive in that awful weather is still unfathomable to me. However, I do recall how exotically beautiful the glistening snow was covering on the ground!

Fortunately, we didn't stay in Alaska long enough for us to freeze to death. We only stopped long enough to refuel and transfer to another plane. A couple of hours later, we took off and headed for California. California became our home for two more days before finally lifting off toward our appointed destination, Houston, Texas.

Our flight arrived late that night and I was amazed as I stared out of the plane window at all the bright city lights below. I couldn't help but think, "Wow, America is spectacular!" As we made our final approach I was enthralled by the magnitude and array of different colored lights. I couldn't help but think, "This must be what heaven is like!" I found myself being enveloped with new hope for our new lives in this great land of America. I thought, "How wonderful it is to be able to come to this great place!"

We were both frightened and perplexed as we stepped out of the plane. We didn't have a clue where to go or what to do. Much to our relief, our family, as well as the other families traveling with us, was warmly and lovingly welcomed by a host of strangers. These cheerful Americans honored us with many friendly smiles and dozens of hugs. They made it a point to affectionately embrace each one of us. The best we could do, however, was smile back, since none of us knew a word of English.

Eventually we were driven to our new home. Can you believe that on my first ride on the streets of America, I got so sick that I threw up all over the van? What a horrible way to show my gratitude to those loving folks. It was then that I realized that I would do better by not sitting in the back seat of a moving vehicle. Since then I have made it a point to sit in the front seat by a window. I suppose the lesson I learned was a small price to pay for my chance to live a better life, but the one who had to clean up the mess may not have felt that way.

I didn't know much about the people who met us that night but I later learned that they were associated with the Catholic Church. They were the ones who sponsored us out of the refugee camps to come to America. One thing that I do know for certain is that God used those loving people to initiate His purpose for our lives. God, in His infinite wisdom, knew that we needed to be in a country like America. He knew that we needed to be in a land where we would be able to experience the influence of Christianity and learn that the one true and living God was Jehovah and not Buddha. He knew that neither Cambodia nor Thailand would provide the kind of opportunity we would need to be exposed to the biblical teaching we would need. So, He brought us all the way from the killing fields, over oceans and continents, to reside in America, the land of the free. What an amazing God; a God who could orchestrate the intricate details of our lives even before we knew Him well or how to ask for His help.

"Let all the earth fear the Lord; let all the people of the world revere him. For he spoke, and it came to be; he commanded, and it stood firm. The Lord foils the plans of the nations; he thwarts the purposes of the peoples. But the plans of the Lord stand firm forever, the purposes of his heart through all generations. Blessed is the nation whose God is the Lord, the people he chose for his inheritance"
(Psalm 33:8-12).

We arrived at the old white house where we were going to live. We were warmly greeted by the other refugee families that were already living there. Although we were packed in like sardines, we all thought it was great. It was hard to imagine that life could get any better. We were so relieved to finally be settling down. Now we could begin to put down new roots in this new land in a house that wasn't made out of twigs and straw. But the one thing that we were most thankful for was not having to look over our shoulders and run for our lives from the Khmer Rouge. As far as we were concerned, we were living in paradise.

Ironically, we arrived during the biggest gift-giving holiday of the year. God was so good to us! An American Christmas was beyond my wildest dreams. I felt like the windows of heaven must have been opened wide. People began to lavish gifts on us. I had never seen such kindness displayed from strangers before. Their kindness went far beyond anything I could have ever dreamed! I remember them taking our family to their church and ushering us into a large room that overflowed with nice second hand clothing and other gifts. We were told to pick out anything we wanted. We were like a bunch of wild eyed children in a candy store as we literally ransacked the riches that were laid out before us. I specifically remember searching for pretty yellow and purple fitted knit tops and brightly colored shirts and shorts. Besides being able to pick out our personal treasures, we also received brand new gifts like dolls, food and even money. While we appreciated the new things we received, we were more than satisfied with our handed-me-down inheritance.

I recall another incident when someone who was living in the house with us gave grandma a delicious granny-smith apple. We had never seen an apple before. We were so delighted to have been introduced to such a fruit. We waited excitedly for grandma to cut the fruit into six pieces, one slice for each of us. As we each took our first nibble into this new exotic fruit, we marveled at just how good it was. We loved it because it reminded us of our green, sour mangoes. Since then, granny-smith apples have been a regular part of our family grocery list.

God truly bestowed countless blessings upon us in our new land. We were not only provided lavishly with the material necessities of life, but we were also exposed to a different kind of love; a love that was undeniably genuine. We became involved with the church's Cambodian ministry and immediately joined their children's choir. I always enjoyed singing in that choir. Singing always brought much needed refreshment to my young soul. While I did not know God as my personal Savior at that time, I really believed that He was the great and mighty God that had saved us from death. So, from out of a deep appreciation as my nine-year-old heart knew, I joyfully sang from the bottom of my thankful heart. I learned, through the lyrics of those songs, that I should give Him honor and praise for all He had done for my family. I don't think grandma would have given me another option, regardless of how I felt. But fortunately she didn't have to coerce me. I sang willingly, with a grateful heart, giving Jesus praise for all that He had done!

The quality of our lives in America was drastically different from life as I knew it in Cambodia. To me it was as different as heaven and hell. I've always compared the Cambodian refugees coming to America to the children of Israel going into the Promised Land. Like the children of Israel coming out from the captivity of Egypt, God delivered thousands of Cambodians out of the oppressive and deadly hands of the Khmer Rouge or slave masters.

It's beyond my comprehension how often God's blessing flow to people that do not claim Him as their Lord and Savior. Then, as I was writing this, it dawned on me that God's love is unconditional. We don't deserve it and certainly can't earn it. His love flows purely from a heart of infinite goodness regardless of our actions, behaviors, and beliefs. His love would not be unconditional if it depended on our action or our reaction toward Him. But because His love is based solely on His holy nature and character alone, this makes His love unconditional to us all. God is not just the source of never ending love; God is love!

For the Lord your God is God of gods and Lord of lords, the great God, mighty and awesome, who shows no partiality and accepts no bribes. He defends the cause of the fatherless and the widow, and loves the alien, giving him food and clothing. And you are to love those who are aliens, for you yourselves were aliens in Egypt. Fear the Lord your God and serve him. Hold fast to him and take your oaths in his name. He is your praise; he is your God, who performed for you those great and awesome wonders you saw with your own eyes"
(Deuteronomy 10:17-21).

The neighborhood in Houston, where we lived, was considered a slum. The crime rate there was extremely high. Every morning, I would hop up on the couch and, through the window, watch while all the action was taking place. Needless to say, our neighborhood was filled with pimps, prostitutes, rapists, drug dealers and murderers. As a matter of fact, a rapist, just few doors down from us, was shot to death for attempting to rape a young Cambodian girl. It was almost like living in a war zone all over again, only this time it was right here in America.

Because none of us knew a word of English, school was very difficult. Because we were poor and had not yet learn about proper personal hygiene we were regularly picked on by the other kids at school. I often wore boy's clothes to school because I simply didn't know any better. My one and only dress was white chiffon. Grandma found it in the dumpster by our house. It had some holes in it but she patched it up and I wore it often.

It seemed to me that I was despised by my classmates which made going to school very difficult. I dreaded going every morning and having to face, again and again, their harsh rejection. But even in the midst of all that humiliation and persecution, God graciously gave me one person who was kind to me and helped me make it through each day.

I became known to many as a troublemaker in my neighborhood. It goes back to rage that still burned deep inside my tormented soul. I didn't hesitate to start fights. My foul mouth spewed out venom on anyone and everyone who dared offend me in any way, shape or form. It was so grotesquely vile that grownups were left speechless. Grandma was at a loss. She couldn't discipline me hard or fast enough. Not even her belt could curb my tongue. Because of the fires that I set off with my unruly tongue our family actually had to move from home to home.

After living in Houston for about a year, we decided to move to Florida so we could be closer to other family members. Grandma and my aunt decided that it was best for all of us to be closer, since grandma and grandpa were getting too old to take care of us. So in late 1982, our family of six got on a Greyhound bus and headed for Lakeland, Florida. Their daughter, also a Cambodian refugee, had been sponsored by St. Paul Lutheran Church in Lakeland. She and her family of five had lived there since 1981. The move proved to be a wise decision. After all, if we had stayed in Houston much longer, I would have undoubtedly made the country's top ten most wanted list.

With the help of their church, our aunt was able to find a small house down the street from where she lived. We were ecstatic! This became our very own home without having the rooms packed full with other families. Grandma must have been relieved hoping she wouldn't have to endure any more shame because of the trouble I'd caused. The little white house on Rebecca Lane in Lakeland, Florida, brought much comfort to all of us.

I immediately fell in love with the warm, tropical climate. It was similar to Cambodia. At our new church there were many wonderful people who showed us love and compassion. We made some wonderful friends there who had a substantial influenced on our lives. People like Mr. and Mrs. Jackie Wilhelm, Mrs. Jane Neirman, and Omar Dittmer and his wife Gladys invested in our family in so many different ways. They were indeed a God send to us.

Shortly after settling in our new domain in Lakeland, Florida, we were approached by our new American friends with the need to change our names. I guess, for the sake of others, we needed more common names so that everyone could more easily identify us. After all, we were in America! Perhaps our names were just too strange and complicated for our new American friends to learn. They were having a hard time remembering which one of us three girls had which name, so they suggested that we each have an American name for convenience.

I remember having mixed emotions about it. I felt disappointed, hurt and sad but then I thought to myself, "Well, I've lost everything else already, what's losing my name? This should be the least of my concerns, considering all of my other tragic losses in life!" So, I went along with our friends' recommendation like the rest of my family. My name, Lakhina, became Linda. Sopheak became Pete. Undoubtedly, our new names were much simpler for everyone to remember.

However, I don't believe any of us had the slightest clue of what mental, emotional and psychological change we would undergo for agreeing to make that critical decision. For me personally, something happened once I signed on the dotted line and bid farewell to my identity of being a "Lakhina" in order to become a "Linda."

I believe once that took place, there was a death of some type that occurred in me emotionally, psychologically and maybe even spiritually. I truly felt I had lost something that belonged to me and was given to me as my birthright. The frustrating part of it all was that I felt like there was nothing I could do about it. After all, I was just a child. No one listens to a child or cares how they feel. I was disturbed and somewhat sad. My name was all I ever knew of me!

"Who is this Linda that I am to become?" I wondered. I was hurt and confused in inexplicable ways. Somehow, I began loathing myself, the "Lakhina" that I was born as. After it was all said and done, I felt as though as I was just a pathetic Cambodian refugee. I became bitter and ashamed for being born into a race as insignificant as mine, the Cambodians. I was angry that I was helpless to change any of my circumstances. After all, I was just an insignificant ten-year-old orphan girl.

We were all so worthless that no one cared to even learn how to pronounce our names. Maybe it was because we were so invaluable that the Khmer Rouge, our own people, was able to exterminate one fourth of our own race. I came to the conclusion that I was born into the most wretched, weakest, useless human race on the planet.

I was a Cambodian. There was a shameful pain that I was not able to express during the transition of losing my identity as "Lakhina." Even if I did know how to express my hurt and disappointment, I wondered who would understand the twisted complexity of my muddled emotions concerning such an insignificant transition like a name change. Who would even care to listen?

I coped with this painful change in the same manner I had coped with all of my other hurt in the past. I took it as another loss, and suppressed my grief as far down as I could, burying it along with my past losses in the sea of despair. There was no time to deal with pain. With a new name, I had to keep up with the new demands of my new identity in my new world, whatever they were! I ignored my pain, confusion and rejection and accepted that "Lakhina" no longer existed. Nothing about her mattered anymore because "Linda" was here to stay!

Lakeland had so much more to offer than any place we had been in the past. In Lakeland, I felt I was able to somewhat live my life as a child finally. I played as a child and laughed as a child. Joy and happiness were once again beginning to overtake the sorrows of my past. I made many friends in church and in school. God gave me the most wonderful fourth grade teacher named Mrs. Wizda. She embraced and nurtured me when others shunned me for having lice in my hair. Mrs. Wizda even took me to Walt Disney World with her and her family. What an experience that was for a young refugee girl to be able to see all the marvels and magic of Disney for the first time!

One of the fondest memories of my childhood in Lakeland is of a precious woman of God who loved my family very much, Mrs. Jackie Wilhelm. I will always remember how she often came to pick all of us children up in her blue station wagon. Then she would drive us to her home and let us play freely in her swimming pool. She made us peanut butter and jelly sandwiches when we got hungry.

Oh, how we all adored Mrs. Jackie! To me, she was an angel sent from heaven. I had never known anyone so kind and so lovely in all my childhood years. Her dazzling smiles would send waves of comfort that delighted my heart with overflowing joy. Her affection became God's mighty healing balm for my deprived soul. I will be forever grateful for her and others like her that God had brought into my once-parched life.

Unfortunately, I also have haunting memories of living in Lakeland that most of my family never even realized. While some knew about the dark secret, they chose to totally ignore it. Others assumed I had manipulated the truth to cover up my horrible behavior. But regardless of who thinks what, the truth, whether it is pleasant or evil will stand on its own.

I guess you could say that as a child I lived a double life. One side of my life was full of pleasures, including kickball, bike riding, fishing and staying over nights at my best friend Tammy's house. These are the priceless memories that I still cherish about my traumatized childhood. I am so very thankful that I have them to recall.

However, the other side to my life was very dark and shameful. My other life was filled with pornography and sexual defilement introduced to me by my step-grandfather. It was an appalling life hidden away from the rest of the family. It began when I joined him at his work in Kau-I-Dang. It followed us to Texas and then to Florida. It was a secrete life of dirty magazines and pornography videos. To most of the family it was a secret, but not everyone.

It was one of my family members, however, that brought that contraband to my step-grandfather. What that family member did not know was that he was sharing that sleazy trash with me. I recall that from the time I was nine years old until I was twelve, sitting by grandpa's bed and looking at that filth with him. He would whisper his sexual fantasies to me; things he would do to me once I was big enough. He would remind me time after time; "Soon, you'll be ready!"

I praise God that time never came. Shortly after I turned twelve I began to experience an overwhelming feeling of shame. I believe it was like the shame that Adam and Eve felt after disobeying God and eating the forbidden fruit. It was as though a light bulb began to illuminate the darkness. For the first time, I saw clearly that what I had allowed my step-grandfather to do to me all those years was wickedly wrong. I felt so disgusted and so ashamed of myself. Like so many young girls before me I believed it was my fault. I remember thinking, "How could I have been so naughty and so wicked to have believed that what he was doing was alright for all those years?"

Hindsight tells me that it was the Holy Spirit that opened up my eyes so I could see that evil for what it was. From that moment on, I knew I could no longer continue to practice that disgraceful, disgusting lifestyle with grandpa another day.

To be honest, I never had the courage to confront grandpa. I was simply too ashamed to be near him. I just made it my utmost priority to avoid him at all cost. I refused to be left alone with him. If the family was going to the store, I went with them. If grandpa went along, then I would stay home. I just couldn't stand the thought of being left alone with him ever again. I couldn't look at him in the face and our house was too small to hide.

I can't tell you how often I rehearsed the scenario, in my mind, how I would tell my grandma. But I just couldn't bring myself to tell her something so shocking. Many times, when he was molesting me, a desperate cry echoed from the pit of my soul, "Please help me, grandma! Please forgive me, grandma!"

But I was never able to tell her about my inner torment. I was afraid that if she knew, it would break her precious heart. I could not bear the thought of me causing her more pain, not after all that she had suffered already. I became a prisoner to my own thoughts and a fugitive in my own home, with no safe place to hide from grandpa.

Grandpa quickly figured out that I was no longer his little playmate. Once he saw that I was dodging him at every opportunity, my rejection made him angry and he began treating me harshly. I was demoted from being his favorite girl, whom he used to lavish with gifts, to his detested enemy. He would show his dislike for me during the times when Sopheak and I got into our sibling brawls. In the heat of our quarrels, grandpa would yell out to Sopheak, "Kill her! Kill her!"

Grandpa will never know how deeply those death filled words wounded me. These were words of hate, from the one whom I had so adored, and they only made me feel more worthless and utterly rejected and betrayed. Once, I truly believed that he was the greatest, most wonderful man alive. Since daddy was captured grandpa had become my substitute Prince Charming and I had been captivated by him and had utterly believed that he truly loved me. But when I heard him shout such words at me I suddenly realized that grandpa couldn't have loved me. He never loved me like I loved him. I realized that his kind of "love" for me was based on conditions. The man that I loved and adored like my own father had betrayed me. I had not been an object of his love but rather an object for him to use. No matter how badly I wanted grandpa and me to be at peace with one another, I could not allow that sick kind of relationship to continue.

Ironically, the very precautions my daddy tried to put in place to protect us from being abused by mother's future husband proved to be wasted. Yet, how could daddy have known that his own stepfather would turn out to be the very predator that would victimize his precious children? How could daddy have known, when he went to his mother for help that he would eventually leave us in the very hands of a sick pedophile.

How could daddy have known? Grandpa had more than one face! The face that most people knew was the carefree, humorous story teller. This was the face that I was so mesmerized by and adored. It was this funny face that got me too close to the horrific face he hid behind his popular public masks.

In my terrible grief I became very angry with God. I'm quite sure my absurd accusations toward Him grieved His holy heart. Over the years, my unresolved anger sprouted roots of bitterness which began to suffocate the tenderness of my soul. If only I had cried out to God in the midst of my hurt and shame! I'm sure I would have received His comfort, but I failed to do so.

Instead, I began to accuse God of being heartless. I blamed Him for all the evil that had taken place in my life. My image of God was now being filtered through a rage-filled heart. Otherwise, I would have been able to see, through the eyes of faith, His goodness. If I had known the truth of God's timeless Word, I would have understood that it was Satan, the father of perversion, who influenced and controlled grandpa. It was Satan who stole my innocence through my grandfather's hands.

Since the Bible says that God is the same yesterday, today and tomorrow, I have no doubt that He tried to show me that He was for me and not against me. I am convinced, if I had given him the opportunity, He would have shown me that He was the answer to all of my pain and that He was the One that could erase all of my shame.

After all, it wasn't God's fault that I ran to my step-grandfather's arms searching for unconditional love. God did not whisper into my longing heart that grandpa would fulfill all of the longings of my empty life. God did not tell me that grandpa would love me with a perfect love like my heavenly Father would.

I am more than confident that God must have tried over and over again to get my attention; so that I could experience His endless love and full acceptance. But then, God was a stranger to me. I did not recognize the gentle voice of my faithful Shepherd. I did not know God as my loving heavenly Father who desired to be all to me and more than I had expected from my grandpa.

> *"How great is the love the Father has lavished on us, that we should be called children of God!"*
> (1 John 3:1).

Through my gracious Heavenly Father's unfailing love and abundant grace, He washed me clean from my past. He healed me emotionally, mentally and psychologically from the shame that once engulfed my heart. He restored what was broken and defiled in my life and has made it beautiful and whole again. In His faithfulness, God also gave me a new heart filled with His grace; enough grace to help me forgive my step-grandfather.

In April 2004, by his bedside, I told grandpa what Jesus had done in my life and that He loved both me and him. Before he passed into eternity, I told him that Jesus died so all of his sins and my sins could be forgiven. I left him with a profound joy and deep peace in my heart. I was able to fully forgive and release him from his betrayal and hurt.

As apart of God's wonderful plan for my life, He gave me a husband who honors and cherishes me as his treasure. Tim's tender heart and sincere goodness has restored my once-broken heart and it is now filled with joy. Tears that once flooded my soul with shame and sorrow are now tears of joy. When I stand in the presence of my awesome God and King, I can't help but burst out with shouts of joy. My Savior has lavished His rich love upon me; a love that satisfies my thirsty soul and fills my heart with a joy that overflows!

> *"'For the Lord will ransom Jacob (Lakhina) and redeem them (her) from the hand of those stronger than they (her). They (she) will come and shout for joy on the heights of Zion; they (she) will rejoice in the bounty of the Lord—the grain, the new wine and the oil, the young of the flocks and the herds, they (she) will be like a well-watered garden, and they (she) will sorrow no more. Then maidens (Lakhina) will dance and be glad, young men and old as well. I will turn their (her) mourning into gladness; I will give them (her) comfort and joy instead of sorrow. I will satisfy the priests (Lakhina) with abundance, and my people (she) will be filled with my bounty,' declares the Lord"*
> (Jeremiah 31:11, AMP).

CHAPTER EIGHT

THE ULTIMATE BETRAYAL

We all loved living in Florida, but finances were tight for our family. Since our grandparents were in their sixties and did not know the English language, they were not able to get decent jobs to help support us. All we had was our monthly support from the United States government. As grateful as we all were for this aid, it was nowhere near enough to meet our family's living budget. Only being thirteen years old, there wasn't anything that I could do to help meet the family's financial needs.

Grandma had a son who worked for the social security department in Denver, Colorado. He assured her that our family could draw more money living in Colorado than in Florida. So, even though no one asked us (the children) if we wanted to stay in Florida or go to Colorado, the decision was made to move; a decision I was very much against. I loved Florida with everything inside me. I had made precious friends who loved me and accepted me and I cherished them. I loved the warm sunshine in Florida. I loved playing in the orange groves that grew near our home.

I had heard about the dreadful cold of Colorado. I felt it was despicably wrong for a scrawny eighty pound warm-blooded tropical creature like me to live in a place with such insufferable weather. I had already suffered through that horrific experience in Alaska and passionately disliked the idea of having to do it again.

In my opinion, there shouldn't be anything living in snow and ice except penguins and polar bears.

So, moving to Denver was appalling to me. I dreaded the thought of having to dress up in three layers of clothes, covering myself up from head to toe everyday for seven to eight months out of the year. Who needs all that to complicate their life? My life was already complicated enough! Well, it seems how I felt did not matter one iota, because in January of 1986 we ended up in Denver in the dead of winter.

After arriving in Denver, our uncle helped us get settled and introduced us to a small Christian congregation made up of Cambodians. We were under the watchful care of Setan Lee, a wonderful pastor, whom I highly honored. I was intrigued with the pastor's humble spirit and my captivated eyes could find no flaws in him. Our family became actively involved with the little church and enjoyed fellowship with the other Cambodian Christians. Grandma even volunteered me to sing in their little choir.

She was proud that I could still read, sing and write in Cambodian. I am sure she was interested in showing me off to the others. Evidently, the other children my age, even some that were older, did not know how to read and write, much less sing in our native language. So the elders of the church showed me much preference. They complimented me often and said that I was an intelligent child.

We enjoyed fellowshipping with our fellow Cambodians for almost two years. It was in that little congregation that grandma felt that she found me a life partner. I was fifteen years old. According to our Cambodian custom, that was the ideal age for girls to be married. She and the elders of the church decided that I should marry a handsome young man in the church that they thought was just perfect for me.

He was tall, light-skinned, handsome, smart, kind and an orphan like me. I'd often heard them praise us both on how smart we were. And since we were both orphans, we were perfect for each other, or so they thought. In their minds they were convinced that we were destined to be with each other. I guess they figured that since we shared common misfortunes and loss, we would somehow be able to comfort each other's lonely, orphaned-hearts.

Well, I admit that for two years I had a mad crush on this young man they had chosen for me. But the truth is that, in my fifteen year old heart and mind, I was nowhere close to being ready to marry him—or anybody, for that matter. In my fantasy, I suppose I had dreams of being married to him one day. But the harder my relatives tried to impose their wishes on me the more unwilling I became. It became obvious, that I was neither ready nor willing!

As a matter of fact, as my elders got together, making their big plans for my wedding, they failed to do one important thing—ask if I wanted to marry him. I became so angry I felt as though my blood would boil. I would pace the room as I eavesdropped on their planning session. The more I paced the angrier I became and the more I wondered what I could do to put an end to their nonsense. Then I came up with a game plan. I would simply march into that room and just tell them how I felt. I thought to myself, "I'm going to tell the elders that I am not ready and I cannot do it. That's simple enough!"

Nervously, I walked into the living room where they were meeting. The truth is that I wasn't brave enough to tell them how I felt. So I walked into the kitchen and grabbed a Granny Smith apple out of the refrigerator. They totally ignored me as though I didn't even exist. I was sure that at least one of them would ask me what I wanted or how I felt. To my astonishment, the elders showed no interest in hearing the desires of my heart. I felt downright violated and helpless! Enraged by their insensitivity, I let out a war cry and threw the apple across the room. The apple smashed against the wall inches over their heads. Then, standing there, trembling with emotion I shouted, "No! I will not marry him. If you want to marry him, you marry him yourself!" And with that, I ran out of the house, slamming the door behind me. Well, believe me, I got their undivided attention and the meeting was dismissed. I didn't hear any more about a wedding after that. I got what I wanted!

I know my outburst must have hurt my grandmother that day. In fact, it broke her heart. She and the others thought they were doing me a huge honor by choosing such a wonderful young man. She felt that it was her duty to make sure I would have a good husband who would take care of me. She thought that I should have been grateful.

But to her dismay, and that of the elders who were there, I brought her much shame.

They couldn't believe that I would repay her for all those years of loving and caring for me with such disgraceful behavior. Of course, in that heated moment, I did not realize all this. All I knew was that there was no way I was going to marry anybody at that time. But I also knew that there were consequences I would have to pay for dishonoring my grandparents. So out of fear, I ran away that evening. The tension in our house was too high for me to handle. I saw and sensed that something died between me and my grandmother. I knew that she was done with me. By the hollow look on her face I knew that she had cut me off from her heart. She would no longer make any more investments in my life. My rebellion caused her to break her covenant with her deceased son.

Father had asked her to take care of his children. It was his last wish before he was captured. But because of my rebellion, she broke the promise that she had made with him. In the end, my own grandmother, the only source of security I had known for 10 years had turned her back on me and cut me out of her life. Her choice to disown me was a crushing blow to my heart. The only conclusion I seemed to be able to reach was this, "If my own grandmother can cut me off just like that, who in this world could ever love me?"

Tensions had already been high in our home before that incident. Sopheak and I fought more often going so far as to try to beat each other with mops handles and broomsticks. Grandpa would watch and cheer for Sopheak, "Kill her, kill her!" It bothered me greatly to see the depth of grandpa's bitterness and hate toward me. I know it was because his lustful spirit could no longer have me. Because I no longer allowed him to use me to satisfy his exotic appetite, my former hero would rather see me dead. I was useless to him! When grandma began calling me a "whore and prostitute" as a result of her wrath toward me, my younger brother took the liberty to follow in her footsteps. When my beloved little brother began calling me a prostitute that was the straw that broke the camel's back. It was at that angry and painful moment that I decided my whole family could all drop dead and I wouldn't shed a tear. I was through with them and made a bitter decision to cut them off completely from my heart.

In retrospect, I can now see the demonic influence that worked so fiercely against my family and me. Satan was busy working overtime through his demons of division, deception, anger, rage, hate, lust, betrayal, and condemnation. The sad thing was that we were all oblivious to his evil tactics. Even though I never went anywhere other than to school, church and a friend's home, and was usually obedient to all of grandma's wishes, I lived in constant torment and shame for reasons unknown to me.

Shame and condemnation weighed heavily upon me during that season of my life. I was imprisoned by the accusations and guilt they had placed on me and it became unbearable at times. It just seemed like the older I became the more critical and hateful they were toward me. I felt it was so undeserved.

I've often thought that the reason grandma was displeased with me was perhaps she had discovered my hideous involvement with her husband. Other than that I couldn't understand why she would treat me as though I wasn't trustworthy and why she called me such terrible names. I concluded that she must have been angry with me because I had allowed her husband to molest me all those years. I wondered why she would call me a "whore" when I was nowhere near being one. But I guess I'll never know.

Satan never thinks twice about making deadly accusations and attacking the nature and character of God's precious children who are created in His image and after His likeness. After all, he is the "accuser of the brethren." Satan was only taking advantage of our ignorance and the sinful nature of my severely dysfunctional family. While I was made to believe that I was hopelessly unruly at age fifteen, I can see clearly now that I was not unruly at all. I was considered unruly because I wouldn't submit to marrying the man my family had chosen for me.

The tension in our home finally got so bad that I decided that we needed to part and go our separate ways. I was not willing to live with them any longer and they weren't willing to let me stay. My aunt made some phone calls to our St. Paul Lutheran Church friends in Lakeland, Florida. She contacted our dear friend, Mrs. Jackie Wilhelm, who, on one of their morning walks together, told Mrs. Gladys Dittmer about me.

Mrs. Dittmer remembered me. I was the sweet ten year old who accompanied her to a piano recital. She also remembered the "Yes, Jesus Loves Me" song that I sang in Cambodian five years before at the St. Paul Lutheran Church. It was her church that helped our family, and where we all attended when we lived in Lakeland.

Because of their deep compassion, Mr. and Mrs. Dittmer agreed to take me into their home. Since their children were grown, married, and out on their own, they had plenty of room in their peaceful four-bedroom home for me. Mrs. Jackie and the Dittmers came up with a plan. I wasn't supposed to begin living with them until the next school semester. However, due to serious tension rising at grandma's home, I had to come much sooner than they had anticipated. It didn't take me long to pack. I was ready to start a new life with a new family. My corrosive attitude and hot anger drove me to the place where, as far as I was concerned, Sopheak, grandma and grandpa no longer existed. They were as good as dead to me.

I'll never forget what happened the day before I left for Florida to be with the Dittmer's. Sopheak came to me and said, "All we have is each other, please take me with you! There are only two of us, we need to stay together! You are my sister and I am your brother, please let me go with you!" Deep down in my bitter heart, I longed to believe that his plea was sincere and they were his words. But, I knew that a close friend, Knor, who loved both of us dearly, told him to say those words to me.

My little brother's pitiful pleas set off a major struggle in my heart. One part of me wanted to soften and allow him back into my heart. I deeply wanted to believe that those were his words. But I wouldn't allow him the benefit of the doubt. The door of my heart had already been slammed shut and sealed.

I had been hurt and disappointed too many times and I would not allow myself to become vulnerable with him or anyone else. It was too late! He had betrayed me and sliced my heart into pieces when he called me a "whore." How could I forget those spiteful words? That wound was too deep and fresh. The damage had already been done. My mind was made up—I would never love or trust anyone again.

So, out of my deep pain came my terrible response. It is hard for me to put those horrible words down on paper. But at that moment, they spewed out of my mouth like bullets: "You are not my brother and I am not your sister! We are nothing to each other and I do not want you to come with me! I hate you and I wish you were dead!"

I have no idea what happened after that; I honestly cannot remember. With all the hurt and anger coursing through my anguished soul, my words were like sharp nails to his heart. However, as fate would have, the next day both he and I boarded a plane and flew out to begin a new chapter of our lives. However, it was with separate families. Sopheak went to live with my aunt's family and I was headed for the Dittmer's home.

CHAPTER NINE

WHERE DO I BELONG?

One ordinary evening, Mrs. Dittmer opened up her backdoor to find a teenage orphan girl standing there with a suitcase in hand. Up until that time it had been, no doubt, just another peaceful evening at the dinner table. As the door was swung open I could tell that she was surprised by the look on her face. She wasn't expecting my arrival so soon but, never-the-less, she called out to Mr. Dittmer who kindly ushered my aunt and me into their kitchen.

Inside the Dittmer's cozy country kitchen auntie apologized for bringing me much sooner than they had agreed. She explained that things had progressively gotten worse and so they thought it would be better to bring me now. After a brief but informative update, my aunt said her good-byes and left me with my new family.

From outward appearances, it would seem that living with the Dittmer's would have filled my heart with joy and singing. What more could I want? God had provided me with two of the most wonderful people I could have ever hoped to meet let alone love and nurture me. I was in a non-abusive, Godly environment where I didn't have to feel ashamed or guilt everyday. I was in a safe place!

However, in spite of the new, positive environment I found myself not able to enjoy it. I didn't seem to be able to deal with all of my suppressed pain. I was tormented day and night. The questions that kept running through my mind were terribly painful. Who could help me clarify the deep issues swirling in my soul? "Where do I belong? Where is my home?" I remember, one day after school floating on a raft in our backyard pool, staring up at the sky and wondering if I would ever see my homeland again. My heart was heavy as I wondered if I would ever see my mother again.

At night, when I would look at the moon, I would pretend that I could see mother's face looking down at me. I hoped that somewhere, far away, she would be looking up at that same moon. This practice brought me comfort and a connection with her that I desperately needed. I longed for just a glimpse of her but it always seemed to end the same way with nothing but an empty orb beaming down at me.

For the first few weeks I stayed at the Dittmer's, when I laid my head down to sleep on my soft new pillows, a horrible sense of loneliness would surround me. The pain was so great that I literally had knots in my stomach. I felt as though my heart would burst into a thousand pieces. Again, that gnawing sense of being misplaced began to overwhelm me. I seemed to be suspended in a pool of misery and confusion as I cried myself to sleep night after night. One night my grief was so profound that I awoke Mrs. Dittmer. While she did her best to comfort my broken heart, stroking my hair and whispering sweet words she couldn't take the pain away.

I am happy to say that life with my new family did eventually improve. As you can imagine, my coming to live with them demanded changes from all three of us, changes that required adjustments for which none of us could have been prepared. With me came my taste for jasmine rice, fish sauce, and stir-fried jalapenos. Mrs. Dittmer told me that I was to prepare a meal for the family on Thursday nights. Being Asian, my style of cooking was much different from hers, especially where it came to seasoning food. So I just prepared my favorite spicy hot dishes and decided if they wanted to eat on Thursday nights, they would just have to toughen up. Needless to say, there were several meals where I wasn't sure that they would make it. With teary eyes and runny noses, the Dittmers braved my cooking. In fact, I was quite impressed with their determination in not giving up. To my surprise, they were much tougher people then what I had initially gave them credit for.

I lived with the Dittmer's for three and a half years. I truly was blessed to have their guidance and support during those critical years of my life. I needed their support through my junior high and high school experience. They stressed the value of fellowship with other Christian teens and involved me in anything and everything that had to do with church activities. They would sign me up and send me to every activity with the church or its youth group.

I will be eternally grateful for the quality of life that these godly people tried to instill in my life. They were the first ones in my life who loved me unconditionally. Because of their selfless love and sacrifice, they saved me, at least at that time of my life, from turning to a life of drugs and alcohol. There's no doubt in my heart that I would not have made it through my teenage years without these two angels.

Although the Dittmer's lifestyle was anything but extravagant, we lived a good life grounded by their faithful focus on the Lord Jesus Christ. As I look back, I believe my involvement with the St. Paul Lutheran Church youth group represented one of the most positive segments of my life. My wonderful mentors planted godly seed in my life that would eventually reap untold dividends for many years to come.

Eventually, however, I began to feel uneasy that my younger brother wasn't enjoying the same measure of care and security that I was. I eventually learned that, since I have been with the Dittmer's, Sopheak had moved four times and lived with four different families since we had come to Florida. I had been concerned that he might have a more difficult time when he initially moved in with my aunt because she had three children of her own. As caring as they might have been, I knew that if Sopheak got into any type of confrontation with one of their kids or her husband, he would be booted out the door. After all, he was the foster child.

Compelled by my brother's worsening living situation, I finally mustered up enough courage to ask my gracious foster parents if they would consider taking Sopheak into their home. My family ties were too strong for me to do nothing. I couldn't stand the horrible thought of my baby brother moving from one foster home to another like some cast off rag doll. I could see no reason why my wonderful guardians would not accept him.

I reasoned with them that they had two extra bedrooms and that they could give Sopheak the smallest room by the garage. I argued that then we would both be grateful for their generosity. I truly believed the Dittmer's would understand my anguish, but more importantly that they would see my baby brother's need for a home where he could also experience their unconditional love.

After prolonged deliberations, I finally asked them, "Will you please take my brother in to your home?" Their gentle response was not what I wanted to hear, "No, Linda! We are sorry, but we do not feel that at our age we can handle another teenager in our home." As you can imagine my heart was crushed. Almost immediately that ugly voice crying "rejection" returned and said to me, "You are not important and no one really cares about you or your brother. No one truly wants you. You are nothing but a huge burden to people and a waste of their time and energy!" Taking sides with that voice inside my head, I cried out to the Dittmers, "You are just like everyone else in this world—heartless!"

I don't remember if I actually told them that I hated them but if I didn't tell them then, I certainly felt it from the depths of my soul. Their "no" was like a sharp dagger to my heart. I guess my pain was much greater because they were turning their backs on my baby brother. Maybe we couldn't get along very well for long; I did love him with all my heart. To me, he was the only person that I had left in this world. His life somehow became my only substantial purpose for living. My world seemingly shattered as I stormed into my room and cried my heart out one last time at the Dittmer's house. Enraged, hurt and bitter, I closed the door of my heart to my loving hosts.

It was in late August 1990, just after my eighteenth birthday that I walked out of the Dittmer's home. In all honesty, now I deeply regretted leaving the security of their care and the comfort of their love. But because I had believed my own self contrived lies, that these loving people did not care about my brother and me, I refused to continue to live with them. How could I continue to live there believing that they too were rejecting my precious brother?

The Dittmers had showered me with love and kindness for the more than three years. What a way to repay them! Yet all I could think was, "I don't need them. I can make it on my own; without them and, for that matter, without anyone's help! I told myself, "My brother and I will be just fine. We'll be better off taking care of ourselves without heartless adults telling us what to do and then breaking our hearts anyway!"

So finally, Sopheak and I were together once again. This time I made up my mind that I would never let anyone or anything separate us again. Energized with this silent vow, I became determined to seek legal guardianship of Sopheak. I would gladly assumed responsibility, not only as Sopheak's big sister but as his legal guardian as well. Sopheak was sixteen and in his junior year at high school and I was just beginning my senior year.

We were both attending Lakeland Senior High School at the time when I assumed responsibility for both his and my well-being. I was more than willing to do whatever it took to ensure our safety and future. In reality, we became our own caretakers. We both agreed that our need to depend on others was now part of the past.

Because money was scarce, we were forced to move to the rougher side of Lakeland where we found a one-bedroom apartment. Sopheak demonstrated his chivalry by giving me the bedroom while he slept on the couch. We shared the rent, the food, the light bills and everything else that was needed.

In order to make ends meet, we worked at two different Chinese restaurants. The owners saw that we were industrious workers and very responsible so they gladly left the running of both establishments to us. Motivated by our need to make money, we fervently took to our new jobs. After all, we were on our own and had more than adequate share of bills to pay. We each worked on an average of about sixty hours per week. This was on top of our full-time school schedule. So, between managing our school work and the restaurants, we had no time for any social life. However, with my brother by my side, I felt that I was nearly invincible and could just about conquer the world with one hand tied behind my back.

Living together in that apartment brought about a much-needed healing to our relationship. The anger and hatefulness that had been so prevalent before immediately began to subside. It seemed as though all our selfish attitudes and the ugly words we used to scream at each other were left in the past for good. I'm sure God had a hand in orchestrating the peace my brother and I began to experience.

Our sibling affection deepened as we began taking personal responsibility for each other. While I can't remember ever sitting down for the express purpose of putting our inner feelings into words, neither of us believed that there was the slightest possibility for anyone to ever destroy that special place we held in each other's heart. Sopheak literally became my primary reason for living. Nothing came close to motivating me other than taking care of my brother. I loved him with an unending devotion.

Sopheak graduated from Lakeland Senior High School in 1992 a year after me. We were ecstatic over this wonderful accomplishment. "We made it!" In spite of the hardships and challenges of our desperate lives, we made it through our high school together. We felt so proud to be over comers.

Yet never once did we think to give any honor and glory to God, who was the one who ultimately helped us. It was simply out of ignorance that we lavished all of the kudos on ourselves for making it through those hard times. We were arrogant to think that we did it all on our own. I can almost see a slight smile form on God's face as He watched us celebrate our accomplishments.

Graduation meant the beginning of a new life for Sopheak. It soon dawned on me that my little brother had dreams of his own; dreams that did not include me. In my mind I thought that we would be together forever; always ready to watch each other's back. I was in no way prepared for the devastating announcement that was soon to come. It just never occurred to me that we would ever be separated. After all, I left everything; the comfort and security of my foster parent's home to take care of him. I had vowed never to let anything come between us again and I had assumed that he felt the same way toward me. Was I ever naïve?

I vividly remember that chilly day as my beloved brother shared with me his lifelong dreams. He said, "Sis, I have always wanted to follow daddy's footsteps. I want to be a soldier, just like him!" I can still see him as he passionately shared his life's aspiration; to be what daddy was, a soldier and a hero!

While he was pouring out his dreams, my heart sank! I thought, "This can't be happening. You are all I have left in life. How can I lose you, too?" But I was too overcome to share my troubled thoughts with him. How could I discourage his exciting dreams with my selfish needs? While Sopheak never truly knew daddy something inside of him wanted to be like him. Our daddy had become a hero and a legend to him through the many stories told about him by our family. Now, my young hero wanted to follow in the footsteps of his hero father.

Putting aside my personal disappointment, I remember a sense of pride rising up in me. Imagine my little brother pursuing such a risky career—one that could very well cost him his life just as it cost our father his life. I was honored that he wanted to be like daddy. But deep down inside, I shuttered at the thought of loosing him in the violence of war. How could I ever face that reality? What would happen to me if he was taken from me like daddy? Could I take it or would I loose my mind? For me, losing my little brother, whom I loved so much, might be the final straw.

After all those horrible scenarios finished winding their way through my mind I heard a familiar voice. "See, even your own baby brother doesn't love you enough to stick by you. There he goes, turning his back on you like all the other people in your life." Those thoughts had tortured me relentlessly. How many times had I faced other moments like this when I was forced to deal with my self worth? Again, I surrendered to another lie. My heart sunk under the terrible pain of betrayal and abandonment. Once more, I was going to have to face life alone, without Sopheak to whom I had given my heart.

How could he do this to me? I had been his protector since we were children. I was appointed to protect him from the world even when we fought like wild dogs among ourselves. The betrayal was deep, too agonizing to utter. There was a part of me that did embrace his decision to join the United States Army, but depression had submerged my heart as I thought about how I would soon face life without him by my side. Drowned in my own pity and sorrow,

I could only fake an ounce of affirmation to celebrate my brother's bravery for pursuing his ambitions.

I didn't have the courage to express my true feelings to him about my personal pain. Rather, I tried my best to convince him that I was strong and that I would be okay with him gone. But just beneath the thin veneer of my manufactured smile ran violent streams of anger, hurt, and loneliness. And once again, I found myself nearly destroyed by feelings of abandonment.

How I would face life without my brother? I felt like a ship, adrift on an ocean without a compass. What was my place in this large, lonely world? Just where do I belong? What is going to become of me? What will I do with my life? Do I actually have a purpose in life? Over and over I wrestled with these tormenting questions. For the most part, they became the agonizing refrain for my troubled heart over the summer of 1992.

CHAPTER TEN

ANGELS UNAWARE

Nineteen years old and free at last! Oh, life in the big city! Orlando was the place to be, so I lived in Orlando bouncing from home to home for about ten months. I worked at a Chinese restaurant in downtown Orlando as a hostess during the weekdays and partied from club to club at night. I made friends with a Korean girl, named Tina. She came from an abusive family and had run away from home. She was a fabulous dancer who was very talented and a lot of fun.

We became inseparable as we seemed to cling to each other for dear life. We spent most of our time hopping from Vietnamese restaurants to nightclubs week after week. I guess our orphaned hearts bonded us together. We were both drifters, victims of the vicious cycle created by a lonely and rebellious life.

Neither of us had a clue about what we were going to do with our lives. Personally, I couldn't see myself going to school considering the little bit of money I was making. I had just enough for rent, car insurance, food and nightclub expenses.

My aunt, who lived in Denver, Colorado at the time, felt that I was wasting my young life away. So, she invited me to move there and attend college. To pay for my tuition, she promised to help me apply for a Pell Grant. Being in college herself, she saw that partying in Orlando would only lead to a bleak future. I knew that she was right, so I sold my car, packed up my bags and flew to Denver. It was very difficult for me to leave Tina all by herself in Orlando. But I felt that I needed to make the right decision for my future.

So in January of 1993, I returned to cold, dreary Denver, Colorado. Just as planned, my aunt helped me enroll at the Arapahoe Community College at the foothills of the Rocky Mountains. The initial plan was for me to stay with her and her boyfriend. But their apartment was too small for all three of us so I stayed across town with my uncle and two cousins. My uncle was hardly ever home. Like my father, he was addicted to gambling. That kept him in the casinos every evening till four o'clock in the morning. I shared his house with my two precious cousins who became very dear to my heart. With their father gone most of the time, we were pretty much on our own.

In order to support myself through college, my aunt suggested that I get a job at Hooters. She told me that Hooters girls make great tips and it looked like a lot of fun to work there. She kept after me for weeks until I finally told her "Why don't you go work there if you want me to work there so bad?" But we both knew that she was too inhibited and could not handle an environment filled with flirting men. She had always been the quiet one while I was known for being outgoing and outspoken.

But what she didn't know was that I was very insecure about how I looked. I hated what I considered my fat cheeks. It actually made me feel unattractive and repulsive. I've always despised my wide Asian face. Besides, I figured I needed a large pair of "hooters" to work there. So, I resisted her requests simply because I felt that I did not have what it took to be a sexy Hooters girl. But my aunt finally convinced me that if I wanted to make great money while going to school Hooters was the way for me to go.

Finally, she pumped me up with enough hope and courage to walk through Hooters' front door and ask for an application. I was so timid and embarrassed that I walked through the restaurant with my head down, staring at the wooden floor the entire time. I met the manager, whom I mustered up enough courage to look directly in the face, and asked for the application. I sat at the bar and filled out the application and turned it in once I was finished. To my shocking surprise, I was hired that day as a Hooters girl. I just couldn't believe that he hired me, a short girl with an average-sized chest to be a Hooters girl. But both my aunt and I were thrilled that I got the job.

I worked at the restaurant during the day and went to school in the evening. I hated going to that school with a passion. Because I had no car and had to take a city bus, going to my classes was drudgery. I also hated the dismal weather. But I knew I needed an education so I forced myself to endure my situation. Actually, I was delighted that I listened to my aunt about working at Hooters. I did make great money and, at the same time having what I thought was fun. All the attention I received fed my deprived soul and gave me the affirmation I so desperately lacked. I worked for the Denver Hooters for six months.

Six days after my twenty-first birthday, I had a harrowing experience that would forever alter my view on life. Before my experience, I had no fear of anything or anyone. Somehow I had come to believe that I was truly invincible. Because of this illusion, I became careless with my life and the choices that I made.

On August 9, 1993, I was getting off work sometime around midnight. I called my boyfriend to see what he was doing. I had wanted to go out with him, but he told me that he was going camping and fishing with his buddies. He had offered to pick me up from work and drop me off at home before leaving, but feeling rejected by him, I told him no. Some of my fellow employees also offered to give me a ride home, but out of prideful independence I refused their generosity. I justified my decision on my belief that I didn't need to depend on anyone and was certainly capable of getting home on my own. So I took the city bus as usually. I can't remember how many times my boyfriend and others had warned me that it wasn't safe for an attractive young female to ride the bus so late at night. But stubbornly, I rejected their wisdom and headed straight for the bus stop.

While waiting, with the other passengers for the bus to arrive, a large white man in his mid-thirties with shoulder-length dirty blond hair struck up a conversation with me. While he was big he was not intimidating but seemed peculiarly tender and compassionate. In fact, he looked somewhat out of place. While there were many people at the bus stop, he was the only one who spoke to me.

He asked me in a pleasant tone of voice, "What is a pretty young girl like you doing at the bus stop so late at night?" I told him, somewhat condescendingly, "I just got off of work, and I'm going home!" Then he proceeded with what seemed to be a mild warning. "It is not safe for you to be out on your own this late at night! There are many evil men who roam the street at night who might do you harm."

I was somewhat taken by his evident concern, but I firmly reassured him, "Nothing is going to happen to me!" In my mind I was thinking, "Oh, please! I've survived much worst things in the Killing Fields than riding the bus late at night!" I reassured the stranger that I was not afraid and I would be fine. I was touched with his genuine concern for me but it seemed a little extraordinary. He was a bit too caring for a stranger; it was as though he was pleading with me to reconsider my choice for that evening.

Convinced that I was untouchable, I hopped on the bus along with the stranger and the others who were waiting with us. He sat in the back of the bus, while I sat closer to the front. He did not intimidate me with his size; I actually saw him as a big teddy bear with a giant heart. Yet, he seemed bothered by the choice I had made.

Less than an hour later, we arrived at my stop. It was a major intersection just two blocks away from my home. I got off the bus and noticed that the stranger also got off at the same stop with me. Now I was somewhat unsettled because I was thinking that he might follow me. But when I peeked over my shoulder to see which way he was heading, I was relieved to see that he was going the opposite direction from me. However, I did sense that he was very concerned for my safety and that he was somewhat burdened in his heart that I foolishly rejected his warning.

Quickly, I dashed across the intersection and headed toward my street. I walked a block away from where the bus had dropped me off. As I was reaching into my backpack to get my keys, I was suddenly grabbed from behind. Startled, I dropped my keys in the middle of the street just four houses away from my front door.

It didn't take me long to realize that my attacker was not the tall stranger. My attacker was a much shorter man and he had a heavy Latino accent. In fact he wasn't much taller than me. Now, here I was in the very situation I had been warned about; attacked by an evil man prowling the streets at night wanting to hurt me. How I wished that I had listened to those who had tried to warn me. More than anything else, I wanted that big stranger to rescue me.

My abductor tried to cover my mouth and began to push me out of the lighted street toward the dark alley behind my house. Now I was really frightened. Pleading with my abductor, I begged him not to hurt me, but he only snarled at me to be quiet. I told him that he could have my money but he just snickered at my pleas. Softly he said, "I'm not going to hurt you. I don't want your money. I love you!" Then he was silent.

His silence painted a dreadful picture of his evil intentions toward me. I realized that this stalker was someone who had been watching me, admiring me, and planning this evil night. It was perfectly clear to me now that I was not, in fact, untouchable. My foolish pride had become my down fall. But it was too late to correct my foolishness for I had fallen into his trap.

It was dark in the alley where my captor pushed me to the ground and began trying to tie my hands behind my back. Then he pressed a dirty cloth into my mouth. At this point I was beginning to lose any hope of getting out of this ambush. In the struggle I thought about the nearby dumpster and was overcome with the thought of someone discovering my dead body the next day.

Like flipping pages in an old album my thoughts wandered off to my beloved brother, Sopheak. He was now serving in Kuwait so very far away from me. My heart sank at the thought that I might never see him again. At that moment, my one great desire was to see Sopheak and tell him just how much I loved him.

While I've always loved him more than life itself, it was never easy for me to express my feelings for him. I thought to myself "I cannot leave him without first letting him know how much I love him!" While my mind was on thoughts of Sopheak, my stalker was preparing himself for his sexual escapade. Once more, I pleaded with him not to hurt me, and his response was the same: "I'm not going to hurt you, I love you!"

It is hard to explain how utterly alone I felt in that dark alley in the grasp of a beast that was about to violate me. Looking up I saw the twinkling stars. They seemed to ignore me, unconcerned about my desperate situation. I could hear my next-door neighbor's television. He often stayed up late watching his favorite show. At one point, another one of my neighbors turned his back porch light on to try to see why his dog was barking. Either unable to see anything in the pitch black alley or afraid of what he might discover, he went back inside, once again leaving me abandoned to the merciless hands of my assailant.

The only faithful witness I seem to have was the neighbor's dog that kept up his persistent barking just on the other side of the fence. It was as though, in some way, he was aware that a crime was taking place. His barking began to arouse something deep within me; a kind of instinctive courage that began to bubble up in my spirit. Somehow, my new furry friend made me feel as though I was no longer alone with the rapist. The barking dog suddenly became my champion; a cheerleader right there beside me; a witness that could see what was happening to me and didn't like it. The commotion he was making fueled me with courage and strength to fight back.

While the rapist was making preparation to appease his sickening appetite, I was preparing myself for a counterattack. I knew that I would not have much time, perhaps only a fraction of a second to act. When he took his filthy hands off of me to unzip his pants, I knew it was my golden moment to get free. It was now or never! In his feverish lust driven resolve to have me, he failed to bind my hands securely. The very second he took his hands off me, like a lightening flash, I bolted up from my position, dashing through the alley as fast as I could. I began screaming loudly, hoping that one of my neighbors would hear me and come to my aid.

Free from the rags that he used to tie up my hands and mouth I continued to run up the street toward my house. I let out a blood-curdling scream until I was breathless. I quickly learned that running uphill in the mile-high city was no easy thing and I lost my voice within seconds. As hard as I tried to scream, I couldn't make another sound.

I ran straight to my house in hopes of finding my uncle or cousins there. After banging frantically on my front door I realized no one was home so I went next door and banged there. No one home there either. Paranoid, I crawled behind the shrubbery at my neighbor's front door. I sat alone in the darkness, afraid for my life. I had enough presence of mind to remove my shiny jewelry and belt buckle and stash them beside me. I was worried that my attacker would find me if he saw their reflection.

While hiding there, I saw a small car moving about half a block away. It had its lights turned off. I was almost certain it was the rapist leaving the scene. But I was so paralyzed by fear that I wouldn't leave my hiding place. I did see the neighbor across the street come out of his house. I guess he was wondering what all the commotion was about. He turned on his lights, walked outside for a short moment and then went back inside. Not sure if my attacker was still looking for me, I stayed in that bush for nearly an hour.

Finally I crawled out of the bush, ran around my neighbor's house, and jumped over two fences to the far side of my house. I found another bush and crawled under it. Another hour must have passed while I waited for either my uncle or some passerby to take me to the police station. Finally, a couple of hours after the attack, a car came by. It was a family of four who were delivering newspapers. As they came near I dashed to the middle of the road and flagged them down. Thankfully, they took pity on me and drove me to a nearby gas station so I could call the police.

Once the police came, they took me back to the crime scene to investigate the incident. We found the rags that the attempted rapist used to tie me with. My backpack was still left untouched and so was the money. We walked over to the intersection where I was first abducted and found my keys lying in the middle of the street. But at the time, because it was still so dark, the police were not able to find any other clues. As a result, they said that they would return in the morning to do a more thorough investigation.

It was after four o'clock that morning when my uncle returned home from the casinos. He pulled up in front of his home to find a crime scene complete with police cars. After I shared my terrifying experience with my uncle, I told him I did not feel safe staying in his home any longer. I shared with him my sixth sense that my attacker knew exactly where I lived and had been stalking me for some time. I was afraid that he would not give up and would try to attack me again.

Having experienced this frightening assault, I never looked at life the same way again. The darkness inundated me, especially if there was the slightest crack in my curtains. I obsessively pulled down all of the shades, but could not shut the rapist out of mind. I was inundated with the feeling that my assailant was on the outside of the windows peeking in at me, the same way my step-grandfather used to peek into my windows. So I called my boyfriend to come pick me up from my uncle's house that same night.

A few days later I returned to my uncle's house to pack up my things. I told my aunt, who lived in Florida what had happened and she invited me to relocate and live with her. Only this time, she had moved to Fort Lauderdale, Florida and was sharing an apartment with her fiancé. Within a week of this incident, I was again in Florida, this time in Fort Lauderdale, launching a new life.

I've had a long time to think about that horrible night. It has only been recently that I've been able to see things painted through the Word of God. God tried to teach me a very important lesson, a lesson I wish I had learned immediately after the attack. But I didn't. I was too stubborn, too prideful, and too hardheaded to understand what my loving Heavenly Father was so interested in trying to teach me. I was a fool who thought I knew it all. But according to the Word of God, I knew nothing!

It took me a long time and I had to face numerous painful experiences before I finally began to understand; before wisdom finally begin to filter through my brain. Because of my lack of understanding, I almost perished. But again and again my merciful Heavenly Father created ways for me to escape death in spite of foolishness.

In retrospect, I know that He warned me not only through ordinary people like my boyfriend and co-workers, but even through that caring stranger. It is not difficult for me to believe that the tall fellow who spoke to me at the bus stop was one of God's angels on a mission to warn me of impending danger that night. Not only did he seem peculiar and out of place, but his genuine concern for me was one of sincere compassion that is not usually found in an ordinary stranger. Perhaps I will never truly know, but deep down inside my heart, I believe that God did send my angel to try to warn me of the trap that I was about to walk into.

"For wisdom will enter your heart, and knowledge will be pleasant to your soul. Discretion will protect you, and understanding will guard you. Wisdom will save you from the ways of wicked men, from men whose words are perverse, who leave the straight paths to walk in dark ways, who delight in doing wrong and rejoice in the perverseness of evil, whose paths are crooked and who are devious in their ways. For the upright will live in the land, and the blameless will remain in it; but the wicked will be cut off from the land, and the unfaithful will be torn from it" (Proverbs 2:10-15, 21-22).

God mercifully rescued me from the evil plans of my assailant. Thank you merciful God for your never ending goodness! Through that ordeal and many others, I've learned to embrace the value of obeying Your voice of wisdom. The Word of God says that, "for wisdom is more precious than rubies, and nothing you desire can compare with her" (Proverbs 8:11).

CHAPTER ELEVEN

A DEAL WITH THE DEVIL

*G*oodbye, dreary Denver! Hello, tropical Florida! It was in late August of 1993 that I flew down to join my aunt and her fiancé in Fort Lauderdale. I was more than delighted to be back in my favorite state. Fort Lauderdale was so much different than any place I had ever lived. It was a tropical paradise and a setting for me to live out my fantasies. It was the place to live for any young person who thrived for life in the fast lane. Once again, I got a job at the Hooters closest to where we lived. And it was there that my reckless lifestyle would eventually overtake me.

It didn't take long for me to discover and begin to experience the vain lifestyle of the young people I met. I noticed that all of them, guys and gals, were what I call very "high maintenance." But I guess a more accurate word to describe of my new friends was clearly "shallow." Most of the girls I worked with were into artificial nails, hair extensions and breast implants. To me it was really mind-boggling! I had never used fake nails. In fact, using them had never entered my thinking, much less, fake breasts. But, in Fort Lauderdale, it seemed to be the norm. It seemed cosmetic surgery was as common as buying a new pair of shoes. And the guys I began dating were as "pretty" as the girls. What I mean by that is most of them shaved their legs, got manicures and waxed their eyebrows. I had never seen anything like that in my entire life.

The girls I began doing special promotions with quickly brought me up to speed regarding whom to date. They only dated guys with hot bodies, fast cars, and of course, lots of money. Initially I though the lifestyle of my new friends was shocking. I actually remember saying to God, "Lord, please don't let me become like them. They are the phoniest, most materialistic and shallow people I've ever met!" It wasn't that I felt that I was any better, I was just different. Even casual acquaintances would tell me that I was different. And it wasn't that I was part of a minority, it had to do with my disposition; how I thought, my values and work ethic as compared to my peers.

Almost immediately, I found that working at Hooters in South Florida was much more fun than the one in Denver not to mention the tips were better. I was really baffled at how eager men were to throw their hard earned cash at me in exchange for a little bit of attention. Undoubtedly because of my exotic appeal, I was constantly in demand for marketing promotions. We did numerous professional golf tournaments, Miami Dolphins games and professional hockey tournaments in the Fort Lauderdale and Miami areas. Once again, my tropical appeal brought me favor in the eyes of my management team and on two occasions I was asked to consider being one of the Hooters swimsuit calendar girls. Although my pictures didn't actually make it into the calendar, somehow, being in the top three chosen for the photo shoot really gave my low self-esteem a much needed boost.

Because working hard was a high value to me, I quickly found favor with my managers. They notice that I was dependable, fast, polite and highly attentive to my customers and my responsibilities. It wasn't unusual for me to work six days a week. In fact, I often worked my shift and the shifts of other girls who would call in sick. Because I was financially challenged, I didn't mind. Actually picking up all that overtime really motivated me and besides it was something I enjoyed doing very much. One of my highest priorities was to purchase my own car. I didn't have parents to buy me a nice condo or a new sports car to drive like many of the other girls. So, for the first few months at Hooters I kept myself focused on saving for a car.

While I appreciated my job, little did I realize how working for Hooters would eventually cause such unbelievable problems in my life. Although I considered myself a good person with great personal qualities, the values of the people I worked with eventually began to erode my values. I soon discovered that I was thinking and acting like them. At that time in my life, I was unaware of the valuable instruction God provides in His Word regarding the kind of influence those we associate with can have on our lives. This lack of knowledge nearly destroyed me.

"Do not be misled: 'Bad company corrupts good character.' Come back to your senses as you ought, and stop sinning; for there are some who are ignorant of God—I say this to your shame"
(1 Corinthians 15:33).

For the first year I lived in Ft. Lauderdale, I pretty much stayed within bounds, and I didn't party excessively like my friends. That was partly due to the fact that I had a boyfriend. He had won the Mr. South Florida pageant and my relationship with him kept me home. Those who knew me would, no doubt all agree that I lived a relatively normal and balanced life. I worked regularly and had even enrolled part-time at Broward Community College.

Inspired by Kiana, an attractive Hawaiian body building celebrity featured on ESPN, I spent a great deal of my spare time in the gym. Hoping to look like this TV fitness idol, I was obsessed with maintaining a toned physique. In fact, I was often mistaken for Kiana by many people, which elevated my ego straight off the charts. I also discovered that the gym was where many young chiseled bodied bachelors went to work out. Who needs nightclubs when there's a gymnasium filled with hot men sporting buffed bodies and gawking at you? Even with all the distractions, I was able to work out and flirt a little bit as well.

Finally it seemed that life was going well for me. I thought, "I am finally living the good life. What more can I ask for? How could it get any better than this?" At that point in my life there was no place I would have rather been and there was no one else that I would have rather been than me!

After about a year of being what I thought was the preverbal "good girl" I decided it was time to venture out and taste the wilder side of Fort Lauderdale. So, I said my goodbyes to Mr. South Florida and traded him in for the freedom and opportunity to date the other attractive men. I truly cared for him, but I didn't care for his obsession with marijuana. I consistently refused to join him because I found it basically repulsive. Sitting home at night with him was really becoming boring especially when I knew that there was an exciting world out there just waiting for my arrival.

When I finally did make my break with him I was like a wild animal without any restraint. For me, life truly began at nightfall. Fort Lauderdale provided a variety of nightclubs to choose from. The blaring music, the glitz and glamour, and of course, the stares from guys, seemed to electrify my soul. It wasn't long before a couple of nights of weekend fun turned into three, four or as many as five nights a week. It didn't take me long to adopt the persona of a popular professional club hopper. My new life was both exciting and addictive. I was too busy making the most of my new life style to understand why the club scene held such appeal to me. In retrospect, I realize that it was the perception of popularity and the immediate attention and affirmation from the men that constantly surrounded me that my attention starved soul was longing for.

The emotional and physical depravation of my childhood and the lack of consistent love and affirmation created a deep need in my life. I perceived myself as being an outcast, poor, and unattractive. Now this newfound popularity made me feel important like a spoiled kid in an ice cream store. I was no longer rejected but accepted, especially by the opposite sex, but even some female friends as well.

I mainly dated men from the NFL and other professional sports leagues. This really boosted my low self-esteem. I was offered impressive materialistic things from expensive cars and the keys to their condos. While my ego soared my enormous pride and lack of trust kept me from accepting any of their gifts. After all, I didn't want my boyfriend from the NFL to think that he could own me. I wasn't about to accept such luxuries if I was going to be perceived as his "girl." I was determined to play hard to get!

In actuality, my insecurity and fear became my defense. No one was going to break my heart if I could help it. My heart had already been broken so many times; I was unwilling to allow myself to be vulnerable with anyone or settle down with any one. I needed to be in control of my heart. Besides that, since there were so many options, I could afford to play hard to get.

The truth of the matter was while I thought I was outsmarting them by playing the field, I was only hurting myself. In the end, I realized that playing people is a two way game. I was also being played, used and defiled. The joke was on me!

I lived this lifestyle in the fast lane for five years. All I lived for was immediate gratification, with no thought of the consequences. However, in June of 1997, at the age of twenty-five, my promiscuous life style finally caught up with me. At first, I had no idea what was happening to me. But it wasn't long before I realized that at sometime in the process of "playing around" with my many boyfriends, I had conceived a baby. My first thought was, "Which one of my boyfriends does this child belong to and what in the world am I going to do with a baby?" The thought of becoming pregnant had never crossed my mind. But evidently I was a much bigger fool than I realized.

I was scared out of my mind. I thought, "I can barely take care of myself. How in the world would I take care of another human being? What do I know about taking care of a baby or raising a child?" Bombarded with these horrifying questions, I began asking advice from my friends. My manager told me that his baby girl was the greatest thing that ever happened to him. It was evident that he was crazy about his daughter. When I expressed my fear of being able to provide for the baby, he told me not to worry, that there were a lot of programs available to help single moms like me. I reminded him that I would be completely alone raising this child and I did not think I could do it. I mentioned the possibility of abortion and he counseled me that it was not a good choice.

I also sought advice from my closest girlfriend. She was a single mother of two and had had several abortions. She flatly told me, "If you keep this baby, you and I are through." She told me that the only reason she hung out with me was that because I attracted men, associating with me provided a prime opportunity for her. Can you believe that? I am amazed at how desperately foolish I was to settle for such a shallow friendship.

I can't believe that I had stooped to such a low level of "friendship." What we had was an association not a friendship. I can't believe how gullible I was. I guess my own low self-esteem blinded me to reality. Perhaps that was the very thing that drew me to her in the first place. I became a willing participant in her selfish terms for friendship. I guess I believed I did not deserve any better in a friend.

I knew that I didn't have to ask my boyfriend about keeping the baby. I knew beyond a shadow of a doubt that the moment should I decide to keep the baby he would ditch me. Besides, I wasn't sure if it was even his baby. So how could I have confidently expected him to desire the baby? There was no way that I could have ever been brave and honest enough to tell him that I'd been playing around behind his back all that time. Then we would be through for sure! I had somehow during years of self-destruction become too weak and dependent to be happy without him. Simply put, I was too fragile, broken and shattered to stand confidently on my own. I felt that I couldn't live without him and that I needed him.

On the other hand, I knew my pregnancy was the most disgraceful thing that I could ever do to my family, especially knowing that my child was the offspring of an African-American father. From our experiences of living in the ghetto of Houston, Texas, many of my family had formed an extreme prejudice against African-Americans. I had clearly seen their reaction to my cousin's pregnancy by an African-American. So, I knew beyond the shadow of a doubt that choosing to keep my baby meant rejection by what little family I had left.

Desperate and torn, I sought advice from one of my dearest family member. After she had listened to my concerns and fears, she advised me to go ahead and abort the pregnancy. Being pregnant and not married would have brought much disgrace to our family among our Cambodian community.

I have to admit that the possibility of having my own child truly did thrill me initially as I contemplated what to do. I began dreaming of how nice it would be to have someone to call my very own, someone that would be a real and intricate part of me; flesh of my flesh, bone of my bone. I thought perhaps having a baby would take care of the inner cries of my heart, a heart that yearned so desperately to belong to someone so that I would feel significant and valuable.

Somewhere in the depths of my heart, there was a small hope that maybe having a child would finally complete and heal the loneliness that had been gnawing in me all of my life. Outside, I appeared to be so tough, independent and lacking nothing. But just below the surface was a heart that desperately cried out for love, affirmation, and acceptance. This child might be just what I needed.

But I didn't have anyone who was close enough for me to talk to; to share my strange irresistible idea. I couldn't tell my brother. I was afraid that he would reject me. I would never be able to handle rejection from him. So I did what I had learned to do best. I suppressed it and disregarded it as a blissful fantasy. How could I have been so foolish, to think that I could keep this baby for myself?

The cold hard reality was that I knew nothing about taking care of a baby or raising a child. Actually, I had always been deathly afraid of having to watch little babies. How could I ever forget my little baby brother, Bountho, who died under my care? And how could I ever forget the little baby girl I was so nervous about holding at the age of eleven and whom I had accidentally dropped on the floor?

Besides those gruesome facts, I was bound by the fear of rejection from the most important people in my life: my boyfriend and my family. The pitiful hidden weakness I faced was a horrible fear of rejection. Having lived my entire life deprived of real love and acceptance as an orphan my heart had already reached its limit. I decided one more painful blow of rejection would literally kill me.

Therefore, I made a vow to myself. As difficult as it was for me to come to the decision, I had convinced myself that I would not allow another human being to suffer rejection like I had suffered. I was determined that my child would not know that kind of pain. I thought I was trying to shield my precious baby from pain but my vow was nothing more than a death sentence for my unborn child. After thoroughly weighing out my options over several very emotional weeks, I surrendered to my fears and made the selfish decision to not face more shame, pain, and rejection. I had decided to go ahead with an abortion!

That next morning, my friend willingly drove me to a walk-in abortion clinic in her neighborhood. She knew the drive very well, since she had gone through this several times before. It was easy for her to see that I wasn't very happy about my decision mainly because I did not have much to say to her as we drove. I was anything but my usual cheery self. I was still struggling over the choice that I had made. So, before we got out of the car, she wrapped her arm around me, encouraged me with a smile and tried to get me to brighten up some.

We eventually arrived at the clinic and I signed in with the receptionist. She gave me some paperwork to fill out. Still overwhelmed with what I was about to do, I asked the nurse some questions in hopes of finding consolation. The nurse nonchalantly assured me that I was doing the right thing, and that I would not remember a thing once I woke up. With her half-sincere assurance, she hurried off to do her chores. Fretfully, I went and sat down to wait for the doctor's call.

Finally, they called my name. As the nurse led me into the next room, I saw a number of young girls, lying on mattresses on the floor. Evidently they had gotten there earlier than me. They looked so young; like they were still in their teens, not even women yet. I was shocked to see how many girls had come there for an abortion. All of them had similarly sad looks about them as if something had left them lifeless and hollow inside. Their young faces seemed to be filled with so much anguish. The nurse led me past them as she directed me to go lie down on my bed and wait for the doctor. I guess she could see that I was nervous, so she reassured me that I would not remember a thing once I woke up.

After a brief moment, he came in and gave me a sedative to put me to sleep. He was all business. He had no time for comforting conversation. The entire staff was on a mission to do their pre-appointed task. There were no emotions expressed, just the performance of an operation. The doctor's shot caused me to fall into a fast, hard sleep.

I'm not sure how long I was out but I will never forget waking up that dreadful day. It seemed like the darkest hour of my life! Not long after I regained consciousness I remember hearing what I could only describe as a firm, yet concerned voice. "You have made a deal with the devil!" I knew instantly that it was God's voice. I sensed, for the first time that God was heartbroken with me and that what I had just done had grieved His heart greatly.

Because of my deep guilt, I literally felt as though God had turned his back on me and forsaken me at that moment. Because I did not know about God's promises to never leave or abandon his creation, I thought that God was done with me for good. Believing this lie nearly shattered my heart. From the depth of my soul I let out a deep, mournful cry, "No! What have I done? What have I done? My baby, my baby! What have I done?" I can still remember those cries as they continue to echo through my soul.

I immediately acknowledged spilling innocent blood; blood that was surly on my hands. There was no attempt for justification. I had killed my baby! What could I do now? There was nothing left for me to do. It was too late!

I remember raising my knees up against my chest and rocking back and forth in sorrowful remorse. I cried out, acknowledging over and over again the horrific sin I had committed. I considered myself nothing more than a brutal shedder of innocent blood. I was so deeply depressed over what I had done that all I wanted to do was to die like my baby.

No matter how hard I tried to forget what I had done the unforgiving weight of my sin plunged me into deeper depression. Following this experience, I began abusing alcohol all the more. I began drinking earlier and earlier in the day to try to drown out my guilt and fears. It became the only way that I could cope with each new day; a way to deaden my conscience and the deep pain in my soul. How other people perceived me no longer concerned me. Whether others saw me as someone on the verge of loosing it really never entered my mind. I soon developed a "why should I care?" kind of attitude and refused to look at myself honestly. Even if I was drinking more and more every day, I had always been strong and tough and I would continue to be that way now. I had been a survivor and would continue to be a survivor.

Life became more and more untenable for me. I became unable to grasp any concept of the value of a human life, not mine or anyone else's. Personally, I found that having taken another life devalues all dimensions of life. Life, after all is God's most precious gift. The overwhelming guilt of the abortion had a desensitizing affect on my heart. The wellspring of my life was drying up.

It would be more than five years before I married and conceived another child. That experience helped me understand the greatness of God's grace. Having conceived, I realized that He had not rejected me. The new life within me shouted to me of God's forgiveness for denying life to my first child. Oh, how ridiculously foolish I was! Instead of appreciating and embracing that first baby as His gift, I cruelly rejected the very thing that God meant to use to shower me with indescribable joy and fulfillment.

I now know that babies can help fill the longings of the human heart. However, I also know that there is another place inside our hearts that only our Maker can fill. But now having personally experienced motherhood, I know that that precious child would have brought me much fulfillment in that lonely season of my life. I should have listened to God's voice that tried to whisper gentle warnings to my heart. Unfortunately I didn't know God, nor did I recognize his voice. Ultimately, fear had gotten the best of me!

In spite of my disgusting actions and wickedness toward God, He still chose to show mercy upon me. He did not abandon me. No doubt He was angry and deeply disappointed by my conduct, but He never stopped loving me. Instead of getting what I deserved, He showered me with mercy.

> *"Yet he was merciful; he forgave their iniquities and did not destroy them. Time after time he restrained his anger and did not stir up his full wrath. He remembered that they were just flesh, a passing breeze that does not return. How often they rebelled against him in the desert and grieved him in the wasteland! Again and again they put God to the test; they vexed the Holy One of Israel"*
> (Psalm 78:38-41).

> *"Who is a God like you, who pardons sin and forgives the transgression of the remnant of his inheritance? You do not stay angry forever but delight to show mercy"*
> (Micah 7:18).

CHAPTER TWELVE

SET APART

I wish I could say that having the abortion was the worst choice I made during my younger and more foolish years, but it would not be true. What is true is that I was so traumatized by what I did that it was difficult for me to make responsible choices. As hard as I tried, my life only seemed to go from bad to worse. After the abortion, it was as if the gates of hell burst wide open and unleashed multitudes of demons to influence every area of my life. I became a completely insensitive and empty person. Life became more and more meaningless. Before having the abortion, I was really intent on finding some kind of meaning to life. But after that dreadful day, overwhelming despair and guilt drowned my last desire for life's value or meaning. Weighing barely ninety-five pounds, I had resorted to merely breathing and functioning as a walking corpse. Because I had seemingly nothing to live for, death seemed to loom over every decision I made. Once again, it seemed that the grave was ready to swallow up what little was left of me.

Years of rebellion and wrong choices left me completely incompetent to judge right from wrong. Truth became lies, and lies became truth. I found it more and more difficult to differentiate between good and evil. Making quality decisions became more difficult as my senses were dulled and confused. To simply state it: I wasn't good for anything. Everything I touched seemed to be lifeless to me.

I became dangerous to both myself and to society as well. I became irrational when it came to thrills and adventure. I seemed obsessed with a desire for high-risk action. Defiantly, I bullied my way through life like a Tasmanian devil. I became addicted to the thrill of street racing and it was simply the phenomenal grace of God that kept me from being killed. But in my mind I had nothing to lose.

It didn't matter who I raced because the only thing I was interested in was the adrenaline rush. I would fly over highways at outlandish speeds of up to 130 miles per hour. The interesting thing was I didn't even have to be drunk to pull such stunts! Life was quickly becoming little more than a game. Because I saw no value in it, I lived solely for the sheer ecstasy of one temporary gratification after another. I suppose the early trauma I experienced in the Killing Fields of Cambodia made me impervious to senseless risk taking when I grew up. I seemed to be addicted to the adrenaline rush I got when I was involved in life threatening experiences. But this was only one of several dependencies that controlled my life.

Reckless street racing, men, drugs, and liquor was sending me quickly down the path to destruction. My self-gratifying lifestyle was destroying me from the inside out and I didn't realize it. I'm still amazed when I think about the countless times I was drunk as could be, yet somehow, safely drove myself home. On numerous occasions, I couldn't even remember getting into the car and turning on the ignition to drive home, but somehow, would wake up the next morning safely in bed.

There is only one explanation: It couldn't have been anything less than the grace of God that protected me. My pastor once said, "With some of us, God must have had to send an entire legion of angels to protect us from the destructive plans of the enemy." The only difference in my case was the devil didn't have to try very hard. I was doing most of the work for him. I was definitely way up there on God's "high maintenance" list. His angels must have had to work around the clock watching over me and snatching me out of the countless pits I stumbled into.

"But in your great mercy you did not put an end to them or abandon them, for you are a gracious and merciful God" (Nehemiah 9:31).

Around the time I turned twenty-five, I began to notice a subtle change in myself. I was becoming less and less interested in the things that used to give me a rush. I began withdrawing from the seductive thrill of party life and the revolving door of meaningless relationships. The things I had feverishly run after were no longer gratifying. I didn't know what I needed to satisfy the deep longings of my heart. I had no idea then that what my empty heart was searching for was a meaningful relationship with God Himself.

I just knew that I needed to stop playing around. I concluded that what I needed was to get serious and settle down with a good man. I figured that pursuing a good career and finding a faithful husband, with whom I could give and receive love, would bring me the peace, purpose, and fulfillment for which I so desperately longed.

One spring afternoon in 1998 while I was alone in my condo feeling lonely and empty, once again, I heard that firm yet gentle voice saying, "Come to me, my child!" At first, I thought I was imagining things. Then I heard the tender appeal once more, "Come to me, my child!" Without hesitating a second, I cried out at the top of my voice, "No! Leave me alone! I am not finished yet. I want to live life as wild, dark, and risky as it has to offer. I want to see it, touch it, smell it, and taste it. I don't want to miss out on anything!" After I settled down, everything became quite. I stood there alone and confused wondering who I was shouting at.

Perplexed over this bizarre incident, I concluded that I must have temporarily lost my mind; yelling wildly in my living room with no one there but me. I know I hadn't been drinking or using drugs. Although I had no firm evidence, somehow, deep down in my heart, I knew that I had been yelling at God. I guess it was out of a fear that He would try to control my life that I had rebuffed His gentle invitation. My conclusion was that by giving in to Him, I would have to give up all of life's fun and thrills. I was certainly not ready to miss out on anything that life had to offer me. I had incorrectly concluded that following God's ways would lead to a super boring life. The best of life would be out of bounds.

As I look back over that time in my life, I can see a compassionate God trying to protect me from my dangerous life style and the consequences it would produce. He could see what I could not see. Actually, God was trying to be my invisible guardian. But because I was unaware of what God was trying to do on my behalf, I continued to follow my own plans. I didn't understand that I could get to know God and discover His plans for my life. No one ever told me that the God of the universe created me with an awesome destiny and that I could discover my destiny through reading the Holy Bible.

> *"For I know the plans I have for you," declares the Lord,*
> *"plans to prosper you and not to harm you,*
> *plans to give you hope and a future"*
> (Jeremiah 29:11).

As His presence left me in silence that day, I can honestly say that what was waiting for me was a path of utter darkness. I'm quite certain that my Lord grieved bitterly knowing what I was about to get myself into. Yet, when I deserved judgment, He gave me mercy. What a gracious and glorious God He is!

> *"Because of the Lord's great love we are not consumed,*
> *for his compassions never fail. They are new every morning;*
> *great is your faithfulness"*
> (Lamentations 3:22-23).

After weeks of considering of what steps I needed to take to better my life and secure my financial future, a millionaire friend of mine asked me to have lunch with him. He picked me up in his red hot Ferrari and drove me to Fort Lauderdale's elite adult club, called Pure Platinum. His purpose for taking me out was to introduce me to adult entertainment where he said only beautiful girls were hired. He assured me that Pure Platinum dancers made about a thousand dollars a night and there was nothing wrong with an intelligent young woman like myself dancing for a living. I told him that I wouldn't dance nude, but I would serve drinks as a cocktail waitress.

My friend introduced me to the manager of the club and told him my desire to be a cocktail waitress. The manager was disappointed that I didn't want to dance, but nevertheless, hired me on the spot. He told me I would begin working that week. Although apprehensive, I knew I needed to make some good money fast to pay my bills. Because of all my recent turmoil, I hadn't been able to work at Hooters.

The first few weeks there, I made good money on the few shifts I worked, but as it turned out, it was barely enough to pay my bills. My financial difficulties began to escalate and weigh heavily on my mind. I was in my mid-twenties facing the real fear of financial failure. I knew that if it was going to be, it was up to me! I needed to do something quickly to secure myself financially.

After barely getting by for two months as a cocktail waitress, becoming a dancer suddenly became more appealing; I would be able to make more money. Staff members and even some customers kept telling me that I was a fool for settling for a couple of hundred dollars a day when I could make the big money dancing. So I began the process of negotiating with myself about what to do. I reasoned that I didn't have anyone to answer to and actually no one that mattered would know about what I was doing except me. None of my family seemed to care what I was doing with my life and no one who would go to that club cared anything about my personal moral standard. Anyway, anyone could visualize me nude any time by simply exercising their lustful imaginations. And, after all, who else would take care of me, if I didn't?

Once I justified every scenario thoroughly, I persuaded myself that dancing was a sure way to get ahead financially. I figured that if I was high enough or drunk that dancing would be a piece of cake. So I made my decision to become a Pure Platinum dancer.

The very day that I was to make my first appearance on stage, God mercifully tried to stop me again. The closer I came to my dancing début the more anxious I was becoming. I quickly downed a couple of drinks and excused myself into the privacy of the ladies room. While changing into my exotic costume I pulled out the fresh marijuana joint I had rolled earlier that morning. I took a few hits hoping to try to calm my jittery nerves and ease my conscience before it was my turn to perform. Through dim lights, I took one last look at myself in the mirror wondering who I had become. Standing there, through the smoke-filled haze, I heard that tender voice again, "You are not one of them. I have set you apart. Don't do this!" This time I didn't scream out, but I seriously began to ponder what these words meant and who was trying to get my attention. As I stood there puzzled, I heard another familiar voice that said, "Do you think you're better than any of those girls out there? Do you think you are special?" Overcome by conviction I responded silently in my heart, "No, I am no different than those girls out there; I'm not more special than them!" With that settled, I snuffed out my joint, went onto the stage, and performed for my fans.

*"Before I formed you in the womb I knew you,
before you were born I set you apart..."*
(Jeremiah 1:5)

This is a very difficult part of my life to write about. Without visiting the embarrassing details, I will just say that I danced as an adult entertainer for three days. Deeply ashamed of what I was doing, I tried desperately to drown out my conscience with alcohol and drugs. But regardless of how many shots I downed or joints I smoked, I couldn't shake off the shame. Then one day, unexpectedly, I had no choice but to quit my new occupation.

To my shock, while I was dancing, my live-in boyfriend walked in. Just two days before, when he questioned me, I swore to him that I wasn't dancing. My real awakening came at that moment when his eyes met mine. I knew immediately how deeply I had wounded him and completely lost his trust. I knew I was in deep trouble and I had a lot of explaining to do later that evening. That was the moment I decided enough was enough. I told my manager I was quitting and went to my locker to collect my belongings. I made a decision then that I would clean up my act and get a job where I could work without feeling ashamed.

CHAPTER THIRTEEN

INSTRUMENT OF WICKEDNESS

Late in the spring of 1998, I heard a knock on my front door. I opened it up and to my surprise I was standing there face to face with my brother, Sopheak. I can't begin to describe how thrilled I was to see him! He was driving a brand new red Acura sports car packed to the hilt with all of his earthly belongings. He asked if it would be alright if he moved in with me for a while. I told him I would be delighted to share my one bedroom lake view condo with him. To be reunited with my one and only brother was a dream come true. It would be like old times when we shared an apartment together in high school. He couldn't have reentered my life at a better time. The throbbing pain of my loneliness and confusion had almost become too much to bear. With Sopheak back in my life, my unbearable loneliness began to subside. But like most my dreams, this one also turned out to be very short-lived.

As much as we loved each other, it was awkward for us at times to be around each other so much again. Because our lives had been so tragically interrupted and forced on separate journeys for so long, we truly did not know each other that well. We certainly were not comfortable sharing deep personal things with one another. But it wasn't long before it became easier and we began to divulge the dark mysteries of our voyage of life during the years of separation.

As we confided with each other, I learned that my darling little brother had also been living a reckless life filled with drugs, alcohol, and promiscuity. We learned that we had both been living similar, unruly lifestyles just a few hundred miles from each other. I discovered that he was battling with the same spiritual, emotional, and psychological pain as me which, no doubt, caused him to choose a similar path of destruction. We certainly knew we wouldn't have to be concerned about being judged for the choices we had made.

During all the time apart, I had no clue what he was going through. I just saw him as a super successful car salesman making a lot of money for someone his age. I had always been very proud of him. The few times we saw each other I never saw a hint of anything that made me to believe he wasn't doing great! It was ultimately a relief to know that someone like Sopheak had also walked in my shoes, felt my pain, and understood my emptiness. We found great consolation being with each other. I found new strength in his presence and for a time, began to feel whole again.

Once we had caught each other up with our pasts, it was time for both of us to get serious about our present situation. We were both without jobs and money was running out fast. Sopheak told me that his car payment was past due and he needed $1,200 immediately. He was three months behind on his payments and evidently the new hot red Acura he was driving was way too fast for him. As much as I deeply wanted to help my brother, I didn't have any money to give him.

Pressed with financial needs, we dove into the employment section of the newspaper in a desperate search for new jobs. My desire was to land something entry-level in the medical field. I didn't mind what, as long as it was in the health and medical industry. I had tried many times to get into the medical field, but without any training or medical school background, the doors always slammed shut. But that wasn't going to stop me from trying once more. I would go with whoever was going to let me in the door. And since I was already in my mid-twenties I needed something long-term.

Scanning through the classified ads, I circled a few opportunities. I found one that was especially compelling. It was an entry-level position for a therapeutic massage salon. At the end of the advertisement, it said, "No experience necessary, willing to train." Excitedly, I told Sopheak, "Here's a position at a therapeutic massage salon and they're willing to train!" When he read the ad he told me, "Give them a call. You don't have anything to lose!" With the support of my brother, I picked up the phone and called. Little did we know at that moment, how much that phone call would soon cost me. Once again, out of ignorance, I walked right into the den of iniquity.

What I had believed to be a legitimate business opportunity turned out to be much different than what was advertised. I had never heard of such businesses. I also sensed the owner wasn't telling me the entire truth when we talked. She was careful not to disclose too much information regarding the details of her services. During that interview with the owner, my instincts kept telling me that something was not adding up. But I figured I needed to give her a chance. After all, she was eager to give me the opportunity I needed. And I was desperate for a chance to get my foot in the door of the "healthcare" industry. To top it all off, my baby brother needed $1,200 and I wanted to help him.

It was my first day on the job and I dressed professionally in my black and white suit. I was excited and eager to learn my new occupation. As soon as I walked into the establishment, with barely enough time to put my keys and purse down, the owner grabbed me and pulled me into a dimly lit room. I was shocked at what I saw. Although I had not lived a totally sheltered life, what I saw at that appalling moment blew me away! I will never forget it as long as I live. Before me was a naked man on his hands and knees, barking like a dog. When he stopped barking, he begged me to urinate on him. Bewildered, I looked at the owner for help, but based on the expression on her face, she was obviously expecting me to comply. Disgusted, I ran out of the room to grab my things to leave. However, the proprietor caught up with me before I reached the front door. She grabbed my arm tightly, stared straight into my eyes, and shouted words that pierced me to my core. She yelled, "Who is going to take care of you when you get older? Nobody is going to love you and take care of you as well as I can! You may be young and pretty now, but when you get older, men will use you and leave you, and what are you going to do then?" Seeing that her words were penetrating my frail heart, her tone began to soften as she reached her hand across to wipe the tears off my cheeks. Tenderly, she proceeded to tell me that she would love me as her own daughter and that she would leave me everything she owned if I committed to her and the business. In that moment, when she said she would love me as her own daughter, I came undone in front of her. For so long, my orphaned heart had yearned for somebody to love me unconditionally as their own daughter. So in that desperate moment, her sweet promise of love and faithfulness to me brought waves of comfort over my barren soul. I began to rationalize, "Perhaps this woman could really love me, since she had no child of her own, and she was also a lonely soul like me!" I stood there in the hallway with tears profusely streaming down my cheeks. I was totally confused and torn between the choices that I needed to make. Should I continue to run towards the front door or should I stay to see her promises fulfill? Sensing that I was weakening, she continued to massage her calculating words into my vulnerable heart.

In the end, I believed that she was right! It was true; I had no one on whom to depend. It was up to me to take care of myself and secure my future. Again, she reaffirmed me that she would love me as the daughter she never had and gently wiped the tears from my face. Seduced by her persuasion, I started to believe that she was someone who really understood me. After all, she was reading me like a book! I figured because she had no children of her own, there would be no one for me to compete with. Because of that one fact, I somehow felt that I would be safe with her; that she wouldn't reject me for her own children. Once she saw that I had fallen under her spell, she told me to toughen up and go to work. I made it clear to her that I would not exchange sex for money, but I would massage the clients. She seemed very pleased with my decision to work for her.

For each of the clients that came through her establishment, the owner charged exorbitant fees. She also required all of her clients to pay her girls a high minimum for their twenty-minute sessions. Because of that, I was able to make six hundred dollars on that first day by massaging just a few clients. It was half of Sopheak's car debt! I was astonished to see how easy it was to make all that money in a matter of just five hours. I couldn't wait to get home and show

Sopheak how much I earned. I knew he would be delighted! This certainly turned out to be the incredible opportunity I was looking for; an opportunity to help both of us financially. Securing my financial future appeared to be possible after all!

At this point, I thought my life was finally taking a turn for the better. I had my brother with me. I was making an average of about $2,500 every four days. I couldn't see any reason why Sopheak would not stay with me for a long time. But to my surprise, within two weeks of his arrival, Sopheak left to take a job in Pennsylvania as a camp counselor for some Christian organization!

I had come to believe that he was the only person in the world that could put my lonely heart at ease. All I know was I desperately wanted him to live with me, and when he left, my heart, once again, filled with loneliness and pain. But looking back, although I didn't understand it at the time, I see clearly that he was simply doing what God was leading him to do.

I made more than $15,000, over the next six weeks, working at the massage clinic. I massaged men and thrilled them through my touches; I learned this ability as a child from my step-grandfather. Because I was making fabulous money, I bought two beautiful, although expensive, long-coat Chihuahuas to keep me company. I had hoped that my furry companions would somehow fill my painful heart with joy. The condo where I lived was wonderful, but my two new roommates violated the "no pet" policy. It broke my heart having to sneak my precious puppies in and out day and night. They needed a fenced yard so they could play freely and now I was able to afford them their needs.

The one thing I remember about those few dark weeks of my life is that I felt myself slipping deeper and deeper into the arena of lust and seduction. I began to discover a new power Satan was giving me over those who were entrapped by lust. It was spellbinding. To realize such control over my helpless victims gave me a spiritual high. It was exhilarating to know that I had such control, able to demand anything I wanted out of those men. They were like puppets on a string willing to do anything at my command. They were slaves to sex, bound to their foul appetites, captive and controlled by their immense perversions.

Psychologically, the more control I seemed to have over those desperate souls offset my own low self-esteem. I looked at each one of them as helpless, despicable "low-life's" who were not only desperate for me but totally at my mercy. I saw it as payback time for the many years that my sick grandfather played with me like a little sex toy, robbing me of my innocence. Many times in those sessions, my mind would recount the many times he defiled me as a child. Along with those shameful memories came a string of stinging emotions, like hate, anger, and vengeance. As I looked at each of my wretched clients, I saw my step-grandfather's face in them.

Knowing what I know now, there is no question that it was the Prince of Darkness himself that gave me the illusion of such preposterous power. He seduced me through the lies he whispered into my mind. He would say, "You deserve this power after all the hell men have put you through. They've used you and defiled you and now it's pay back time." I was goaded on in my present delusion by the memory of all the despicable things my step-grandfather said and did to me! Unfortunately, because of all my insecurities, I fell for his lies.

Ironically, I was actually being controlled by the same dark power that I thought I was imposing over my clients. In reality, all of us were being used; we were no more than slaves shackled by the power of sin and darkness. I had become a tool in Satan's hand; he was using me to do his detestable work of demoralizing men.

Satan knows that human beings are made in the image of God Himself. He knows that mankind is the most exceptional of all of God's creation; created after God's likeness and for His own pleasure. Before mankind ever came into being, Satan was the most magnificent of all of God's creation. He was God's chief musician in heaven. Because of his rebellion and pride, God judged him and demoted him from his high place of prestige, and kicked him out of heaven. Since that day when Satan lost his position in God's kingdom, jealousy, envy, and rage has totally consumed him; embittering his heart toward God and His crowning creation, mankind. Through his hatred for God, Satan has tried to take out his spiteful vengeance on the human race. His plan is simple: to steal from, kill, and destroy God's crown of creation.

What better tool to accomplish his demented desires against God's most cherished treasures than finding someone with a wicked heart like his? I was Satan's perfect candidate to carry out his wicked plans. My heart, like his, was also filled with rage, hate, and vengeance. I guess you could say I was a woman after Satan's own heart. I shared his perversions and lust for destruction. So I had made it easy for him. In order to accomplish his evil work, He simply turned me over to my heart's desires.

Nothing brings Satan deeper satisfaction than to see God's creation absorbed in the evil work of demeaning, defiling, and degrading one another. He knows that nothing can wound God's heart more than to see those created in His image devouring and destroying one another. Obviously, Satan was delighted to use me as one of his many pawns to lead others bound by lust straight into the pit of hell.

No wonder my life had deteriorated to such dismal depression and disgrace. This wasn't just a simple case of bad luck. While Satan was behind me pushing with all his might, I had no one to blame but myself. What put me in such vile places doing such vile thing were my choices and my choices alone. Because God is omniscient (all knowing) He knew, before I was ever born, that I would walk down those very paths. That is why He tried so many times to warn me and invite me to come to Him. He extended His mercy to me over and over again trying to keep me from making such twisted decisions. But I had become a prisoner of my own circumstances and choices; rejecting, time after time, His mercy and His attempts to shield me from a world full of demonic power, lust, and seduction. Just like any loving parent, God was trying to protect me from falling into Satan's horrible trap. But my willful and stubborn heart refused His help.

> *"For although they knew God, they neither glorified him as God nor gave thanks to him, but their thinking became futile and their foolish hearts were darkened. Although they claimed to be wise, they became fools and exchanged the glory of the immortal God for images made to look like mortal man and birds and animals and reptiles. Because of this, God gave them over in the sinful desires of their hearts to sexual impurity for the degrading of their*

> *bodies with one another. They exchanged the truth of God for a lie, and worshiped and served created things rather than the Creator—who is forever praised. Amen. Because of this, God gave them over to shameful lusts. Even their women exchanged natural relations for unnatural ones. In the same way the men also abandoned natural relations with women and were inflamed with lust for one another. Men committed indecent acts with other men, and received in themselves the due penalty for their perversion"*
> (Romans 1:21-27).

I had been working at the massage clinic for seven weeks when the Fort Lauderdale police raided the place. The owner was arrested and taken to the city jail. Fortunately, I had been out of town for a few days and only found out about the raid when I returned. A week later she was released from jail and reopened her clinic. Again the clinic was raided and once again, she was taken back to jail. Only this time, I was there. I was eating some yogurt in the break room when the officers came busting in with their ski masks, artillery, and search warrant. I remember giving them a great big smile while they took my picture. I willingly told them about my association with the clinic.

Because of my ignorance of Florida laws, I had no idea that I was about to be arrested! Furthermore, I was charged for a crime that left me absolutely flabbergasted. As I sat there listening to them, I was shocked to hear that what I had been doing was considered prostitution. I argued, "I am not a prostitute. I was not paid to have sex with anybody. Isn't that what prostitution is all about?" But all they said to me was that I had a right to an attorney. With the citation in my hand, the enormity of my plight began to dawn on me. To my dismay, I realized what grandma and Sopheak said about me had finally come true. I had become a prostitute!

You can't imagine what this revelation did to my self esteem. What little value I held for life completely dissolved. In spite of all the senseless things that I had ever done, being labeled as a prostitute left me feeling more worthless and ashamed than at any other time in my life. It was then that I truly lost hope for having a decent life and I began to be overwhelmed with thoughts of death. It was worse than when I was trying to escape death in the Killing Fields. At least then I wanted to live and was willing to fight to survive. Now I had no desire to put up a fight. I was willing to accept my fate. As far as I was concerned, I was at the end of the road. How could I possibly continue living with the horrid truth of who I had become; worthless to both society and myself?

Where could I ever get the courage to share this disgraceful truth with Sopheak? If Sopheak ever knew the appalling truth of what his big sister had become, it would literally be the end of my life. I was determined to never face my little brother with my hideous shame. I would carry it to my grave before I would ever let my beloved brother know my shameful secret.

Now I really felt trapped. What about my boy friend? I was still trying to regain his trust after he discovered me dancing at Pure Platinum. How could I tell him about the charges against me? It seemed that, from all sides, the walls of my life were caving in. My desperate plight began to plunge me into a deeper depression. While hounded by depression most of my life, I had never come to the place where I was certain that living was no longer an option. Now the shame and the disgrace seemed too much to bear. I wanted out for good. For weeks I began to struggle with thoughts of suicide and began contemplating the best way to end my painful life.

I remember having a conversation with myself one day in broad daylight about a theory I was considering. My profound theory was this: God was not real. He was only a myth. Over and over, like a broken record, I thought, "If there really is a God, then why has my life been so filled with pain and misery? If there is a God, why would he allow me to go through such unspeakable suffering?" So, I reached the conclusion that there was no God! And if there actually was a God, he was not a good God.

Once I had made a final declaration in my heart that a good God did not exist, it seems like death began patiently standing at my door awaiting my final surrender. It was then that I became utterly dependent on alcohol, drugs, and pills to make it from one day to the next. Instead of just drinking two or three drinks a day, I stocked my refrigerator with gallons of wine at a time. I began my mornings by gulping down my wine of choice and smoking a joint till I was no longer able to feel or think about my haunting shame.

Once the high wore off and the pain started returning, I'd call my dealer for something stronger. My supplier would meet me down the street from my house and if he was feeling generous that day he'd give me a freebie; although most of the time, I'd have to cough up twenty-five dollars per hit. But I didn't care how much it cost. At that point in my life, they were more important to me than the air I breathed. Drugs were the only gods I knew that were merciful enough to take away my pain and shame. Every waking moment without them meant that I had to face the demons of fear, shame, and pain alone.

Finally, the day came when it was time for me to execute my plan. There was no point in going on living life the way I was living. I knew I had my precious Sopheak to consider but my desire to end it all was much stronger than my desire to live. I rationalized, "Why would he want a sister as disgraceful as me anyway?" I knew that Sopheak was a survivor; he was strong and smart enough to take care of himself after I was gone. I hadn't looked after him for years, so he would definitely make it without his big sister. I figured he would bounce back after my death and would be able to go on with his life without being burdened and worried about a junkie sister like me.

Later that evening, while I was bathing, I reached for an old razor that had been lying in the soap dish. Flashes of movie scenes flooded my mind. I saw women killing themselves with razors in the bathtubs. It appeared to be the ideal opportunity to go ahead and end my life. That razor had been sitting in the soap dish for several days, so I wasn't sure if it was really sharp. Along with everything else, I didn't want to face the possibility, at the end, of a dull razor blade. Consequently, I checked the blade to determine if it would make a clean and deep enough incision to help me achieve my goal.

I sat down in the tub and wept uncontrollably as the steamy water began to surround my body. In desperation, I tried a practiced run, moving the razor blade over my wrist horizontally, considering how to make the deadly incisions. Hysterical, I began to apply more pressure on the blade. I was afraid to die, but much more horrified to live. In the midst of my agonizing cries a voice spoke out to me,

"Hell is a real place. Don't do this. Hell is real and you don't want to go there!" In unbearable confusion I released a heartrending wail.

After a while and somewhat more composed, I sat there and pondered the words I heard and whose voice it was. I asked myself, "If what the voice just said is true about hell being a real place, then perhaps I shouldn't be doing this. Maybe I need to reconsider." I had heard about hell and I didn't want to go there! Exasperated, I cried even harder. I truly did not want to go to hell, but I did not want to live either.

Overcome by my despair, I was still able to think rationally. "Why should I leave this miserable life here on earth just to suffer all eternity in hell? I would simply be trading one miserable existence for another!" It made no sense to me. Being miserable in life didn't appeal to me but neither did being miserable in hell. It was then that I chose to believe those mysterious words. Although I didn't know God at the time, I was certain that it wasn't the devil that told me that. So I reasoned that the voice was either God's or my conscience.

While it didn't make me happy, I reluctantly accepted the fact that I had to continue my miserable existence. Drowned in sorrow and defeat, I pulled my legs up against my chest and sat there in the tub whimpering like a baby. I thought, "Oh, if only the steam surrounding me would consume me from my existence, then I wouldn't have to feel anymore pain!" But that didn't happen! I simply couldn't find a way to escape.In desperation, I begged God, "Please, whoever you are, just let me die! Please let me die, I don't want to live anymore. I've seen enough evil in this world to convince me that there cannot be a god. If there is a god, he cannot be a good god!" Persuaded by the startling lies of the enemy, the yearning for death became the solitary cry of my heart for the next few weeks. There was no other desire left in me.

His soul draws near to the pit,
and his life to the messengers of death.
(Job 33:22)

The Bible says that the penalty for sin is death. So if that was my rightful punishment it is understandable that the only cry out of my heart in that dark season was to die. My years of unruly rebellion had collected a mountain of debt requiring immense compensation. Satan, the messenger of death, the father of my rebellion, was at my door to collect his due wages. But God, in His love and mercy, was not willing to hand me over to my debtor.

"For the wages of sin is death,
but the gift of God is eternal life in Christ Jesus our Lord."
(Romans 6:23)

CHAPTER FOURTEEN

DEATH INTO DANCING

For the following two weeks after my suicide attempt, I began having dreams almost every single night. The dreams were startling and kept my frantic soul on edge every sobering moment. Even though I was spiritually dead, I knew the dreams had a message to convey to me. The dreams were so chilling that I kept the first few to myself, and just chugged down more booze and pills to try to ignore the intensity of the visions. I was too afraid to tell my boyfriend, because they were grave and deadly. It was a matter of life and death and it involved him, too. I was afraid he would freak out on me if I were to tell him.

I know now that it was God, in His faithfulness, who gave me those soul-rattling dreams. I guess because I was so dense and so lost, God felt He needed to show me them for two consecutive weeks to get my attention. The Holy Spirit was giving me my final warnings to repent through those dreams. If I had chosen not to repent, then the ultimate outcome of my life would have been death, and death was lurking all around me, just as the dreams demonstrated.

To my relief, all my dreams did not end in utter darkness. At the end of many of those dreams, I saw my brother Sopheak, flying a helicopter over to my house to come rescue me. He came to me with urgency, and said, "Come on, Sis, you need to get out of here!" Together, we jumped into the helicopter with my two precious

Chihuahuas and abandoned everything and everyone in my life. I dreamed that Sopheak and I went to Denver, Colorado to start a new life.

Still, after two weeks of clear, intense warnings of the death that I would soon face, I made no changes to my destructive lifestyle. Deep down inside, I truly did want to change. I wanted a new and better life. I wanted a normal, healthy life like the rest of society. But I didn't know how and I didn't have the discipline or the power to live any differently than how I was living.

So, as much as I wanted to change, it was impossible! Instead of putting an end to my sinful lifestyle, the freaky dreams triggered me to drinking, smoking, and popping more pills to mask the dark reality of what might happen to my boyfriend and me. My very last dream, however, did get a startling reaction and response out of me.

In God's rich mercy, He gave me one last attempt to respond to His warnings. The last dream I had shook my senses to the core. I dreamed that I was on the run from death once again. Only this time, the bed that my boyfriend and I were sleeping on was set ablaze with fire. The fire was ferociously wicked and it was engulfing the bed. It was around four or five o'clock in the morning when I saw the vision. It was as though my bedroom was a literal inferno.

Petrified, I jumped out of bed, frantically screaming, "Get up, get up! The bed is on fire, the bed is on fire!" Of course, since my boyfriend and I went to bed stoned, high, and drunk every night, normally it would have been harder for him to get up quickly. But because I shouted hysterically that our bed was on fire, he jumped off the bed like a frog out of a boiling pot. To our sobering surprise, our bed was not on fire at all. As a matter of fact, there was no fire anywhere in the house.

Without a shadow of doubt, I knew that the Spirit of God was making a solemn declaration to me that our bed was defiled. And He was furious with our sins and sexual wickedness, which were detestable in His sight. God not only gave me that dream, but He also gave me the interpretation of it.

It was as though He was saying, "Make no mistake, your behavior and your sin are despicable and you will be consumed like that fire if you don't repent from your wicked ways." With chills infusing my rattled being, my heart was convicted and became utterly fearful of the Almighty God who had spoken blazingly clear to me. This time I knew He meant business. Still, I had no will power to overcome my sinful lifestyle. I was bound to my sins!

For God does speak- now one way, now another- though man may not perceive it. In a dream, in a vision of the night, when deep sleep falls on men as they slumber in their beds, he may speak in their ears and terrify them with warnings, to turn man from wrongdoing and keep him from pride, to preserve his soul from the pit, his life from perishing by the sword.
(Job 33:14-18)

One clear day, out of the blue, there came a knock at my door. It was none other than my beloved brother, Sopheak. Immediately, I knew that the dreams that God had been showing me were becoming a reality. I was so happy to see him. Unlike his other visits, I knew that this time I needed to hide the truth of my circumstances from him, and there was much to hide. I could tell by the look on his face that Sopheak was not thrilled when I greeted him at the door high and drunk, with my ninety-five pound frame half exposed.

After he had observed me for a day, he could see that my daily routine was filled with partying all day, all evening, and into the early hours of the next morning. Although he was displeased with my choice of friends and the boyfriend I was living with, he never said anything. He kept quiet, but I could tell that he was choked up inside, ready to burst with disappointment.

To avoid conflict, he got in his car and took off frequently. He couldn't stand to witness what his beloved sister was associating with and how she had reduced her moral standards. He didn't know how to handle the horrific truth of who I had become. It was too grossly disturbing for him to accept.

I was ashamed because I knew my precious brother could see right through me. Desperately, I had silently hoped that he would just accept me and my choices without any words of condemnation. I was hoping that he would not notice the turmoil and brokenness inside of me. So, I tried dreadfully hard to conceal the disgraceful truth that I was attempting to mask through the excessive drugs and alcohol. The humiliation of facing him with my gruesome reality was more than I could bear.

I just didn't have the courage or strength to tell him where I truly was at that point of my life. More horrendous than that, I couldn't face the fact of who I had become. After all, I was supposed to be the strong one. I was his older sister, the leader, the provider, the one who always had a good, strong head on her shoulders. I was a survivor and a fighter who could stand alone and conquer anything. What he had always known of me was so different from the frail, inebriated half-dead young woman parading in front of his eyes.

I had no concept at that point that Sopheak had become a Christian and dedicated his life to live holy before God. I remembered him calling me on the phone to share his testimony of being saved months earlier. I was genuinely happy for him, even though I couldn't understand his passion for his newfound "religion." Even in the midst of my high and drunken state, I knew whatever it was that my brother had found, sparked a fire in him and it was a positive thing.

But as hard as I tried to understand his zeal for God, I did not grasp the concept of what he was trying to convey to me. I just knew that he was excited and I rejoiced with him because it made him happy. Because I did not understand what being "saved" was all about, I just assumed that he still embraced the familiar things we had shared and enjoyed together from times past. Little did I know that my brother was a new creature, with a new heart and a new life! He was no longer interested in the things that we used to partake of together.

Initially, Sopheak had planned to stay with me for a short while. But because of our conflicting lifestyles, it was impossible for him to be in the same room with me. He tried reading his Bible in the midst of my hedonistic activities with all my decadent, hoodlum acquaintances buzzing in and out of the house. I could tell that he was grieving inside over my worldly, gluttonous lifestyle. But all he could do was get in his car and drive off somewhere to relieve his troubled heart.

One early September day, the week of his birthday, I decided I was going to give him something special as his birthday present. I spent hundreds of dollars on some very fresh marijuana, alcoholic beverages, and expensive seafood in honor of the most treasured person in my life.

I even got my boyfriend, the master joint roller, to roll multiple joints in Sopheak's honor. We were going to lavish him with love, and celebrate his life with the freshest herb around. It was going to be the best party in Fort Lauderdale. It was time to get the party started, so Sopheak and I went into the "dungeon," the dark disco room where my boyfriend was playing his ear-thumping music.

I sat next to Sopheak in front of my ten-foot python cage, lighting up my first joint and rocking my head to the blaring music. The disco lights were flashing and twirling round and round. I wished Sopheak a "happy birthday" and handed him a freshly rolled joint. To my surprise, he turned down my offer. Of course, I was somewhat embarrassed by his rejection.

I went out of my way to buy him the highest quality of marijuana available and he couldn't even appreciate it! I couldn't understand why just a few months earlier he smoked and took ecstasy pills with me and now, all of a sudden, he didn't want to do it anymore. His countenance told me that he was disappointed in me. But I didn't know what to do about it. I figured, "Oh, well. That just leaves more for me!"

We left the dungeon and journeyed out into the kitchen area. I probably went out there to fill up my glass with more wine and he followed me. We sat down at the dining table in the kitchen. While I was puffing and chugging down more drinks, Sopheak looked at me and asked me some profound questions that pierced the center of my being. He looked directly into my eyes and said, "Who are you? I don't even know you anymore. You're not my sister. What have you become?"

It was at that disquieting moment that I realized my brother had found me out. Acknowledging that I could no longer hide, I was forced to peel off the mask that I had been hiding behind. The only person who meant anything to me in my entire world saw right through me. The walls of deceit came crashing down. The dam of my heart burst like a rushing torrent with all the agonizing fear and shame that I was trying to suppress.

Despondently, I confessed to my beloved brother, "I don't know who I am anymore. I don't know who I am or what I am. The only thing I do know is that I want to die. I don't want to live anymore!" I sobbed unashamedly in front of my brother. To be honest with you, I don't remember if he said anything else to me after that. I believe he just sat there shocked and stunned to see his sister dying in front of his eyes. But what I do remember was something so remarkably divine that it has altered the course of my entire existence for eternity.

There in the midst of my anguish, a glowing golden light in a circular form brightly illuminated my dining room wall. The bright glow beamed its vibrant light, captivating my undivided attention. Out of this glorious light came an audible voice, audible only to me and not to Sopheak, who was sitting next to me still in shock. The voice said, "There are two roads in life. You can choose blessings or you can choose curses!"

At that fateful moment, my spirit was made alive. As the scales fell off my eyes, I realized for the first time that all of the horrible things I had lived through all of my life were direct results of my choices and the sinful choices of my forefathers. It was so freeing, at that moment of hearing this, to learn that I was not a victim at all, and that I had total control of the decisions that I made. I did not have to suffer forever as a victim of chance nor did I have to continue suffering for the rebellions of my family and nation. I was the one in control of the blessings or the curses on my life through the choices I would make from that moment forward.

The voice coming from the pulsating light continued, "The thief comes not but to kill, steal, and destroy. But I have come to give you life, choose life! I have always wanted to give you the life that you desired. Come to me and I will give you the kind of life that you've always dreamed of" (John 10:10). The second realization I had was that I was finally able to perceive who the true culprit was behind all the evil and wickedness.

It was not God at all, but it was the devil. He was the thief that slaughtered my people and destroyed my father and my baby brother. He was the one who robbed me of my childhood, my innocence, and my life. It was none other than Satan who had been furiously trying to snuff me out through the Killing Fields up to that point. From the beginning, Satan's evil desires for me were death and destruction.

God graciously had opened up the eyes of my heart to perceive that He was indeed a good God after all! As the God of heaven infused my spirit with His breath of life, He revived me to life and transformed me in His glory! He revealed to me that not only was He the one true and living God, but that He was also my Savior, my Father, and my closest Friend! God also brought back to my remembrance that it was always Him calling out to me to come to Him.

Intoxicated by the presence of a Holy God, I sat there mesmerized by heaven's revelations. With the Maker of my being in my midst, my dark world became fiercely radiant and scattered the demons like terrified cockroaches. As my spirit arose to meet with the Redeemer of my soul, I tasted true intimacy, sweeter than honeycomb, like I've never known before. At that instant, I knew my once deprived heart lacked nothing and no one but God Almighty. I had met the Author of my life. I felt complete and whole in that moment. I was ruined for the ordinary with just one touch from my Master. I knew I was in my King's court, where love, mercy, and forgiveness sheltered me.

God's spoken word to me that evening set my captive soul free from fear, shame, and pain. As God was speaking to me, I felt the shackles of hell around my heart shatter into countless pieces. And miraculously, the horrendous hurt and oppression, from twenty-six years of loneliness, rejection, and abandonment, broke off of me!

> *"You have been set free from sin*
> *and have become slaves to righteousness"*
> (Romans 6:18).

There I was, for a moment in time, face to face with my Creator. Awakened from death unto life, I accepted my Master's invitation to His abundant life. As I made a decision to run into my Father's loving arms, He transferred His compassion into my born again spirit. The King of love and mercy flooded my being with His unquenchable passion to live and tell others about His redeeming grace.

Invigorated by the new life that was inside of me, I ran to the bathroom, locked the door, and shouted praise to my Savior and King. I worshipped, with sheer ecstasy, the God who had set me free. Indescribable joy was released out of my innermost being as I gave thanks and praise to God. I couldn't contain the living water that was overflowing my soul. It was bursting out like a broken dam!

With both hands lifted toward heaven, I jumped and shouted "Hallelujah!" as loud as I could in my bathroom. Surely, with the deafening music and all the action that was taking place in my home that night, no one heard me but God, the angels, and demons. I have no doubts that my shouts of freedom echoed to the throne of God in heaven and pierced the depth of hell at the same time. Satan and his demons must have trembled that night in light of my joyful praise.

The enemy of my soul was undoubtedly furious as God ordered him to release me from his captivity once and for all. The kingdom of darkness lost one of its instruments of wickedness to the kingdom of light. The Holy Spirit and I, along with the angelic hosts of heaven, sang merrily with worship to the King of Kings for His marvelous mercy upon my soul. I celebrated my new life unashamedly before the Almighty!

> *"...he sees God's face and shouts for joy;*
> *he is restored by God to his righteous state."*
> (Job 33:26)

After I had finished singing and shouting, I ran to Sopheak and told him all about the miracle that had just taken place. I told him, "God spoke to me a moment ago. The God of heaven appeared to me in a light and invited me to a new life. I have accepted His gift and I know what I must do."

I proceeded to share with him that God had already told me to leave my home and to walk away from my sinful relationships completely. I think I'm supposed to go to Denver, Colorado, since that's what I saw in my dreams. Sopheak was incredibly relieved to hear my testimony about my divine encounter with the God to whom he had already surrendered. Seeing that his sister was finally safe in

God's protective care, he told me that he would leave Fort Lauderdale early in the morning to spend time with Grandma in Lakeland.

That night, I slept very little. I couldn't wait to get up early to seek God. My soul was thirsty to meet with the living God. He was the Author of my new life and the Source of my next breath. I woke up just before four o'clock; early in the morning while everyone was still sleeping. I grabbed my Bible and went out to the living room. There on my plush ivory carpet, I sat under a lamp to seek God through the pages of Scripture. To my astonishment, for the very first time, the words on the pages of my Bible came alive. It was as though the words had heartbeats behind them. I was thoroughly amazed. I don't know what all I read, but I remember that every thing I read that morning was speaking and breathing life into me. I ate the Word like a hungry, deprived, and impoverished child that had not had a good meal in years.

Spiritually, you could say that I truly was an impoverished child who was deprived of the living Word of God. I could barely contain the excitement as the bible became a newly found treasure that first morning of my new birth in Christ. I had been given the gift of life, which was worth more than any riches the world could ever offer me.

"When your words came, I ate them;
they were my joy and my heart's delight, for I bear
Your name, O Lord God Almighty"
(Jeremiah 15:16).

Out of compassion for my boyfriend and with the passion of Christ in my new heart, I told my boyfriend the next day of my miraculous encounter. I told him about the dreams that I had during those two weeks. I gave him the same warnings that God had given me through the dreams and shared what God had spoken to me about the road to life and the road to death. Boldly, I warned him that God said, "If you don't stop going on this road that you are on, it will lead to death. You will die from the sinful lifestyle that you are living in and you will end up in hell!"

I thought for sure that the revelation I was declaring to him would enlighten his heart and stop him that instant from continuing his sinful lifestyle. I was expecting him to wake up and begin thanking Jesus for saving him from hell due to the knowledge that I was unveiling to him. To my dismay, it didn't quite happen the way I had imagined it would.

He just kept on rolling his joint to smoke, grabbed his usual malt liquor, shook his head, and told me I was going crazy. I was dumbfounded that he did not believe me. I thought, "Why would I lie to you?" I just couldn't understand why he couldn't see that I cared so much for his eternal well-being and that I was desperately trying to rescue him. But I realized much later that my boyfriend couldn't have known God because the god of this world had blinded him completely.

> *"The god of this age has blinded the minds of unbelievers, so that they cannot see the light of the gospel of the glory of Christ, who is the image of God"*
> (2 Corinthians 4:4).

In spite of how my boyfriend reacted to my good news, I knew what I had to do. I was determined to put an end to our relationship and dive in fully to the new life that God was calling me to live. I had to walk away from my sinful life that I was living in order for Christ to live His life in me. After all, without Jesus, I was not living at all. I was only a breathing corpse waiting for the grave to consume me. I thank God for His incomprehensible goodness upon me. He gave me a new, exciting life!

"Therefore, if anyone is in Christ, he is a new creation; the old has gone, the new has come!"
(2 Corinthians 5:17).

"In the same way, count yourselves dead to sin but alive to God in Christ Jesus. Therefore do not let sin reign in your mortal body so that you obey its evil desires. Do not offer the parts of your body to sin, as instruments of wickedness, but rather offer yourselves to

God, and those who have been brought from death to life; and offer the parts of your body to him as instruments of righteousness. For sin shall not be your master, because you are not under law, but under grace" (Romans 6:11-14).

CHAPTER FIFTEEN

CHOOSE LIFE!

"...This day I call heaven and earth as witnesses against you that I have set before you life and death, blessings and curses. Now choose life, so that you and your children may live... and that you may love the Lord your God, listen to his voice, and hold fast to him. For the Lord is your life..."

(Deuteronomy 30:19).

I wish I could say that since I've become a child of God, I have never had any more pain or problems, but that would be absurdly untrue. As a baby Christian, I did fall into another sinful relationship that nearly killed me. But once again, God, in His rich mercy, did not leave me there to die or to suffer the consequences. As certain as the sun rises, once again, He faithfully delivered me from destruction. After I had my fill of doing things my own way, I truly began to taste the fruit of obedience in my Christian life.

In the spring of 2000, I ended a relationship that I had believed to be a God-send. Out of my frustration, I cried out to God, "Lord, I'm tired of my best. Give me your best. I want a man that is in love with You, God! I want a man that cannot live without you, one who loves you passionately without compromise!" Wouldn't you know it? Once I truly desired God's perfect will for my life, God intervened on my behalf.

To make this sweet fairy tale short, God used a stunning lady to introduce me to a wonderful young bachelor in April of 2000. After spending much time observing and interviewing me with her many questions, my future mother-in-law proclaimed, "I have a son that would love you!" Well, the rest is history! God brought Tim into my life just as I had asked. From the moment I saw a picture of Tim's face, my spirit immediately connected with his. Gazing at his photo, the Holy Spirit confirmed with me that Tim was my soul mate and the prince charming I had been searching for all of my life! Of course, I didn't believe it! I couldn't believe it!

One week after meeting his parents, it finally came time for Tim and me to meet face to face. He picked me up from my apartment in Lakeland, Florida and made plans for us to visit some of his special friends in Leesburg, about an hour away. During our ride up to Leesburg, we listened to my favorite worship music by HillSong. We were so comfortable with each other that we sang openly, worshipping God along with the beautiful songs in his Jeep. It was liberating to praise God uninhibitedly in the presence of my special friend. He probably thought I was a fruitcake singing off-key and praising God passionately in front of someone I had just met for the first time. But I didn't care! I was worshipping my Savior for all the things He had done for me.

From the beginning of our relationship, the remarkable spirit and tender nature of my handsome prince swept me off of my feet. No one I had ever known before consistently demonstrated such peace and humility like Tim. He was so different than all those muscle heads and pretty boys that I had once been drawn to and sincerely believed were 'real' men. But after spending that first weekend getting to know each other, I quickly realized that all of those handsome jocks and body builders put together could never hold a candle to my prince. I found, to my amazement, that Tim's gentle strength and confidence was more irresistible than all those muscles put together. For the first time ever, I experienced the joy and comfort of giving my heart entirely to a real man like Tim. It was liberating because I knew that with him, my delicate heart had found a home.

On October 6, 2001, Tim and I were married in his hometown in South Carolina. With special friends and family, we blissfully celebrated our magical night. There was no doubt in our hearts that our divine union was ordained by heaven itself! It was a dream that came true for me to marry such an exceptional man.

Who would have thought that an orphan refugee girl from the Killing Fields of Cambodia would be united with a godly man like Tim who walked a completely different path of life? We came from totally opposite backgrounds. Only God could pull off something so incredible and so impossible! It became evident to me from the beginning that my husband was a huge part of the abundant life that God had promised me. Through Tim, his family, and our precious friends, I have been lavished with love beyond measure. My God has been good to me!

Due to my own severe dysfunction, our first year of marriage was very rough. Besides dealing with our transitions of becoming married, becoming pregnant, relocating to another state with new jobs, entering full time ministry, and looking for a home, we quickly learned that I had deep inner emotional and psychological challenges to overcome. Time after time, I was confronted with the horrible fact that I did not know how to love or trust anyone, including my wonderful husband. I constantly thought of running away from home, our marriage, and from everybody. But I couldn't! I knew that it was God who gave me Tim and the baby that I was carrying. I don't have to paint the portrait for you. For anyone to love an emotionally traumatized woman like I was, with tenderness, patience, and compassion, is not humanly possible! It took the power and grace of the Holy Spirit. Over the years, because of Tim's tenderness, patience, and mercy toward me at times when I was unlovable, he has won my heart over!

Now, five years into our marriage, God has richly blessed us with two incredible sons, a four-year-old and a one-year-old. I realize that my two precious sons are not only gifts from God for Tim and me to enjoy, but they were sent from God to bring healing to my heart. Their lives have caused my heart to overflow with joy and pleasure like I have never known before. Through them, God has taught me what true, sacrificial, unconditional love is. This process of learning to love continues every day. The uncontainable love and joy that flows from my heart for our precious little cherubs has brought much needed healing to my desolate heart. My love and adoration for my children has also revealed much of God's splendid, intimate love for me. As a parent, I can now fathom a facet of the Father's love for His creation; how much pleasure each one of His children brings to Him.

It has been eight years since I accepted the Master's invitation to share in His abundant life. He promised to give me the kind of life that I had been searching for; a life filled with love and not rejection. As you've read in the previous chapters, my life before Christ was filled with pain, shame, fear, loneliness, and confusion. I was so emotionally traumatized that even my own family thought that I was "crazy" and declared me "hopeless." The court system labeled me as "reckless" and "a menace to society." They were right! When the world was so quick in condemning me rather than understanding me, and when I should have been confined to a mental institution or dead, Jesus preserved my life! His love restored my mind and healed my heart.

From the moment I said "Yes!" to Jesus, I knew that I belonged to Him. I understood that I did have a father, and my Father was the God of heaven. This revelation has made me feel complete! I have never had to ask those agonizing questions of: Who am I? Where do I belong? Could someone ever love me unconditionally?

The question that I would like to pose to you is this: Have you found the answer for all of your questions? I've learned that no relationship in this entire world could ever come close to my love relationship with God. You see, the reality of being in love with God, the Lover of my heart and soul, has made me complete. He fills me with satisfaction beyond measure. And because I've learned to put my confidence in His unfailing love, I trust Him to guide me as He pleases. His love and faithfulness has silenced those terrorizing questions and filled my heart with peace. He wants to do the same for you!

"I will be a Father to you, and you will be my sons and daughters, says the Lord Almighty"
(2 Corinthians 6:18).

Because of Christ Jesus living inside of me, I also am able to proclaim that the raging spirits of lust, hate, and anger that once ruled my heart no longer consumes me. Jesus has set me free from these demonic powers. God's love has made it possible for me to forgive those who have hurt me the same way Christ has forgiven me. Everyday, I acknowledge that it is God's remarkable grace that gives me strength to live a victorious life.

God has taught me that my life is no longer my own! My life belongs entirely to Him, for it was He, who saved me from eternal death. God tells me in the Scriptures, that I was made in His image, after His likeness, for His purpose and pleasure. This divine knowledge has freed me from worries and anxiety. The Creator of my being is accountable for every detail of my life. After all, He was the one who formed me and gave me breath. All I am accountable for is to live according to His Word and follow as He leads. Truly, there is no safer place than to be in the hands of the Savior. I've tried it all, and it all led to disaster.

> *"As for God, his way is perfect; the word of the Lord is flawless. He is a shield for all who take refuge in him. For who is God besides the Lord? And who is the Rock except our God? It is God who arms me with strength and makes my way perfect"*
> (2 Samuel 22:31-33).

To this day, God continues to shower His goodness and favor upon my life. All those years when I thought He didn't even care, He was faithfully working out His plans and purposes for me. He even used the evil from my past for His glory. Through this testimony of grace and power, I am compelled to point other orphaned hearts to God's redeeming love. He wants all people to know that He alone is God and that His love for them is infinite! He wants the world to know Him as Creator, Father, Savior, Healer, Protector, and Provider!

> *"I raised you up for this very purpose,*
> *that I might display my power in you and that my name*
> *might be proclaimed in all the earth"*
> (Romans 9:17).

As a young Christian, I thought that Jesus died for me on the cross just so that I would be saved and make it into heaven. I thought that Jesus went through all that suffering just so I wouldn't end up in hell for eternity. While this is all true, this truth only portrays a fraction of my Father's heart. As I grew deeper in the knowledge of God, I realized that He saved my life for a much greater purpose than just me. I've learned that the Father's heart is that everyone of every nation, tongue and tribe would be saved and no one would perish. And He has commissioned broken vessels like me, who He has restored and raised up, to testify of His love and goodness to a dying world.

> *"...because you were slain, and with your blood you*
> *purchased men for God from every tribe*
> *and language and people and nation..."*
> (Revelation 5:9).

He has helped Tim and I give birth to an organization called Legacy of Hope International. The heartbeat of Legacy of Hope is simply to rescue and restore the broken lives of children at risk around the globe. Because of my painful past, it is my life's passion to help orphans, children, and women who are suffering with broken hearts. My heart aches especially for those girls and boys who are exploited and caught in the destructive web of child labor and sexual slavery.

Our vision, through Legacy of Hope, is to provide a safe, nurturing environment for deprived children to learn, grow, and become healthy individuals. We realize that healthy students produce healthy leaders who will lead their generation into building stronger nations. It is the matchless power and grace of God upon my very own life that helped birthed Legacy of Hope International.

Because of what Christ has done for me, I am required to return His gifts of love, mercy, and hope to those who have been abandoned by society. My one true passion in life is to tell the hopeless about the God of hope! I've learned that as I live out this God-given passion to bless others, God also blesses me. Through our outreach in Cambodia, God has reunited me with my long-lost mother. In April of 2004, after twenty-five years of separation between mother and me, our ultimate dream to embrace each other once again, finally became a reality.

But even greater than this, I have had the privilege of witnessing God's faithfulness upon my family in Cambodia. Over time, my family has observed the love, compassion, and goodness of God upon my life. And through our outreaches to the natives in my homeland, many of them could no longer deny the irresistible God that I profess to serve. Today, by the grace of God, both of my younger siblings are now zealously learning to love and serve this great God. Already, they have testified of His goodness upon their new life as children of God. Indeed, they have been forever changed for eternity. There's no doubt that serving God has its sweet rewards!

You've read my life! You now understand that it is only because of God's mercy that I've been led from the killing fields through fields of grace to tell you this story. The fact that I am alive today can be credited to none other than the miraculous power and love of an amazing God! You cannot deny that the God who has restored my life is not a good God. He's an awesome God! I pray that the eyes of your heart will be enlightened to know that there is nothing so horrible, so wicked, and so disgraceful that you could ever do that would stop God from loving you. His love is everlasting and unconditional! His mercy is rich and new every morning. His grace is endless!

One of the greatest lessons I've learned through the darkness of the Killing Fields of Cambodia and all the sin that I've committed is this; the darker the darkness, the brighter God's light shines! The greater the evil, the greater God's power will prevail. I've learned that while it seems there is no limit to the evil of Satan, there is, for sure, no limit to the goodness of God for those in his kingdom of light.

So now, as I close this final chapter, I challenge you to taste for yourself and see that the Lord is good. He has great plans for your life and He desires to bless you beyond your wildest dreams. No riches can compare to God's blessings, for God Almighty is our inheritance!

"No eye has seen, no ear has heard, no mind has conceived, what God has prepared for those who love him"
(2 Corinthians 2:9).

The promises of God are for those who have accepted His Son. To enjoy a satisfying, exhilarating, intimate relationship with a holy God, we must first humble ourselves, acknowledge our sin, and confess that we are sinners in need of a Savior. There is no other way to approach God's throne except through Jesus Christ. This begins with a heart of humility. God loves sinners, but He despises sin! So, to have Jesus come live in your heart, you must renounce sin.

Jesus answered, "I am the way and the truth and the life. No one comes to the Father except through me"
(John 14:6).

Jesus is coming back for those who love Him. I believe with all my heart that the Savior of the world will return sooner than most people think. When He does, He will put an end to Satan and the kingdom of darkness once and for all. And those who belong to Him, God will gather to Himself. Those who do not belong to Him will be destroyed with Satan and his kingdom. My question for you is this: Are you certain that you belong to Jesus Christ? Have you made Jesus your personal Lord and Savior? If you have, then I rejoice with you! But if you have not, then now is the time to accept Jesus Christ as your Savior. You can know beyond a shadow of a doubt that you are saved and that you are a child of God, today!

To invite God into your life, simply say this prayer:

Heavenly Father, please forgive me of my sin and come live in my heart. Reveal yourself to me so that I may know you personally. Thank you for cleansing me with the precious blood of Jesus. I commit my life to you and surrender all that I am to you. From this day forward, please live your life through me. Teach me to walk with you and to love you all the days of my life. In Jesus' Mighty Name, Amen.

If you've just said this prayer and meant it sincerely with all of your heart, Congratulations! You are now a child of God Most High! The Bible says...

"...that if you confess with your mouth, 'Jesus is Lord,' and believe in your heart that God raised him from the dead, you will be saved. For it is with your heart that you believe and are justified, and it is with your mouth that you confess and are saved. As the Scripture says, 'Anyone who trusts in him will never be put to shame'"
(Romans 10:9-11).

For I am convinced that neither death nor life, neither angels nor demons, neither the present nor the future, nor any powers, neither height nor depth, nor anything else in all creation, will be able to separate us from the love of God that is in Christ Jesus our Lord.
(Romans 8:38-39)

LaVergne, TN USA
20 December 2010

209530LV00007B/66/A